I'M THE AMAZING TEI STREET...

WOULDN'T YOU LIKE TO BE AMAZING TOO?

BY:
Tei Y. Street
© Tei Street, 2005

If you have purchased this book with a 'dull' or missing
cover—-You have possibly purchased an unauthorized or stolen
book. Please immediately contact the publisher advising
where, when and how you purchased this book.

Published by StreetTalk Publishing Company
7261 Brooke Blvd.
Reynoldsburg, OH 43068

LCCN: 2005907255
10 digit ISBN: 0-9770009-0-7
13 digit ISBN: 978-0-9770009-0-6
Cover: Design: Marion Designs
Production: Kevin J. Calloway
Editor: Mia McPherson
Author: Tei Street

First Trade Paperback Edition Printing October 2005

Printed in the United States of America

George –

DEDICATION

This book is dedicated to Christopher, Christian, Jonathan, Alli, Natajia & Monte Jr.

-To leave the world better than when we got here, that is the greatest legacy that we can leave.

Thank you for investing in the power that we can build collectively!

The Amazing Jei Stewart

ACKNOWLEDGEMENTS

Recently, I heard Dr. Barbara Nicholson give a speech wherein she declared that she has lived "a perfect life." She explained that Webster's dictionary defines perfect as "lacking nothing essential for life," and continued to explain that her life was perfect because of all of the people who made sure that she lacked nothing essential. These acknowledgement pages are dedicated to those wonderful people who have contributed to making my life absolutely "PERFECT!"

First, I want to thank God because He is the ultimate model of Agape (unconditional) Love (I Corinthian, 13). The sacrifice of His only begotten son, Jesus Christ, demonstrates real love. Because He loved me first and best, I can now walk in love for myself and for others. So, thank you Lord for salvation and forgiveness. You alone are the One who is truly "AMAZING!"

To my parents, I say thank you for the foundation you gave me, for belief in my dreams, sacred trusts and for adopting me when no one else wanted me. Most of all, thank you for raising me up in the way of the Lord and righteousness. It took me a while, but I found my way back to God. Tanya, you were the best sister and role model anyone could have asked for. You are beautiful inside and out. Monte, love, not blood makes us family. I have loved you with my whole heart since the day I laid eyes on you. To Aunt Marion, because you taught us how to play as children and how to enjoy life as adults.

To my "Mifflin Mafia" who kidnapped me from myself. If I live to be 100, I will never really be able to adequately express my heartfelt gratitude to the following women, who as a team, banded together to save my life – Robin Shoemaker, because you rescued me from the system and gave me a home; Sally Kriska, because you put me on the stage and gave me a voice; Dr. Gene Harris, because you helped me to learn temperance and self-discipline while cheering me toward my goals. To my Soror (Sorority Sister), Mentor and lifetime "Other Mother" and friend, Emery Hill, I thank you because you scared me straight, lighted my way, guided me along and never let me give up on me. You taught me how to love me and in doing so, you saved my life. I love you more than this tribute can say.

To my god family, Terry, Christina and Zachary Shields, I say, next to the word "godsend" there has to be a picture of you. For food, shelter, clothing, senior dues, pictures and a lifetime of love I am eternally grateful. I hope your investment in me was worth it to you. You guys ROCK!!!

To Cynthia Zachary-Smith, Ruth Sallee Gresham, and Pat Williams, I say, because of you I know how to mentor other young women. You taught me how to come into my own as a "Sistah," and how to fight tirelessly for what I believe in. The lessons are indelibly etched in my heart and mind. Thank you.

To Siri, I thank God every day for placing you in my life and path. Before you, I never knew what true friendship was. I know that in you, I have a "to the grave" friend. You are the true epitome of sisterhood. And as if that weren't enough, you gave me two magnificent godsons, Ola'seni and Manu. I love you guys.

Sakile Kai, my Sister in Christ and my Soror. Your challenge of me has helped me to grow into middle age. Our path has not been easy, but it has been worth it – every step of the way. Thanks for braving the storms with me.

To my Spec Dr. Dionne Blue, you are the epitome of a true Delta woman. The founders would be proud. You have renewed my faith in sisterhood and given me another Sister to love. Thanks for standing in the gap with me and for sharing your mom with me.

Mary Blue, just when I needed a big sister in life and in Christ, there God was ordaining that our paths would cross. You are remarkable and I feel so blessed to be loved by you.

Terina J. Matthews, you will always be my Delta role model. Who you are and what you have taught me will be with me for the rest of my life. Your sacrifice earned you a lifetime of loyalty and friendship from me.

Kimberly Brant - WOW!!! Though circumstances have diverted our paths, my heart will always celebrate all of who you are as a dynamic DIVA. Thank you so much for your feedback on the content of this book.

To my Sands (special sorority sister who joined when I did), #4 shhhh #2, W. Shawna Gibbs and #12 shhhh #3, Quiona Stephens - you are two (don't get it twisted) of the best gifts I have ever gotten. There is no love like TRIAD love. You inspire me with your greatness and your lack of "self-pity." I know that great things await us because "The Future Lures." Ya'll are THAT DEAL! Delta Sigma Theta Sorority, Inc. brought us together, but love, closets and remixes bonded us for a lifetime.

To Devin, I just want you to know that in me you have a friend and I will always get your back.

To the Black Women's Collective (BWC), I hope you all know that you inspire me to give more, work harder, serve selflessly, and provide opportunities for all of us to net-work.

To Kathy Espy, Les Wright and Joyce Beatty, I thank you for modeling for an entire community of black women what it means to fight tirelessly for what matters. But, I thank you for making the macroscopic lessons microscopically appli-cable by investing in me.

For my Ohio Teen Institute (TI) family, I give thanks because I cut my youth development teeth on TI. Heidi Yoakum, you took me out of a high powered, money making career and helped me to see that true happiness rests in walking in your purpose, not in your paycheck. To Dustine May who gave me my first paid speaking gig, I owe you so much. Thanks to Jodi G. and Marion TI for your faith in me and for always keeping me on deck as a speaker. To my friend Kris Washington who taught me that an old gal can learn new tricks. To Regina Christy and my TI family at "Nor-Nor, Nordonia, you are, you are, Nordonia," your love has certainly lifted me higher. Thank you so much. To the Illinois Teen Institute (Operation Snowball), thank you so much for reminding me that positive messages have a "snowball" effect. I can't name all of the schools and TIs, but just know that you are forever in my heart and my soul.

To my friend, Mr. Chris Corso, thank you so much for always standing for right and for putting your money where your heart is. You are da man.

To the thousands of young people who inspire me every day with your positive choices in the midst of chaotic schools, communities and lives, this book is for you. Knowing that you consider me a role model keeps me humbled and reminds me of my responsibility to and for you.

I will attempt to name all of my nieces and nephews in this paragraph, because whether they came through blood or through love, they are the reason for my work and the future of my family. So, here goes...Syretta, Donnie, Tina, Tony, Kennetta, Deneshia, Lamar, Tiffany, Tameka, Ricky, Taneshia, Tiara, Asia, Michael, Brendan, Brenna, Adrienne, Christopher, Brittany, Tyquan, Marqo, LaMia, David and LaNia.

Finally, this book is dedicated to the true loves of my life, my adopted son/great nephew, Chris, my nephews and nieces Christian, Jonathan, Alli, Natajia and Monte Jr. You are the reason I work so hard. I want you to inherit a world that is filled with love and peace. I know that if it is to be, it is up to me. Never forget that if you put your trust in God and walk in His purpose for your lives, you are the ones who will be truly "Amazing." No matter what, I love you more than air.

Because I believe that it is important to put my money where my mouth, heart and mind are, $1 from the sale of each book will be donated to The Women's Fund of Central Ohio in the names of my grandmother, Ethel Hale, my mother, Theresa Street and my sister, Tanya Tolber. Further, $1 per book will be donated to the scholarship fund of Delta Sigma Theta Sorority, Inc. Columbus Alumnae Chapter, in the name of my Mentor and Soror, Emery S. Hill.

FOREWORD

At the conclusion of each speech, I always found myself wishing that I could have something to leave with the students to whom I had just spoken. So often, students would email me to tell me how different parts of my speech impacted them. They would tell me how much they enjoyed my humor and the wisdom that I tried to impart. One day, a student said, "I wish there were a way that I could get to know you better. I wish you had a book or something that would help me to know more about you." Over the years, I have had a lot of students ask me to put my thoughts on certain topics in a book, so that long after I leave their schools or conferences, they could have something to remind them of the things I said.

For a very long time, I have resisted the request and urge to write this book. Part of my reason for resisting is because it requires me to be much more revealing and vulnerable than I ever cared to be. As you will read in the pages to come, I have not lived the life of an angel. In fact, some have said that my life was just the opposite. For many years I was ashamed of who I had been in my adolescence and in my early adulthood. I was afraid that if I actually penned the words, it would bring all of it back to the forefront of my mind. I was also afraid that my accomplishments would be diminished by my shame. And finally, I was just too lazy to discipline myself to write. So, for the past five years, I just ignored all of the people who asked me to write this book. Then about a year ago, I began to explore the idea of getting the courage to leave my full-time job to pursue my real passion, motivational speaking. I began to discuss the idea of finding a publicist who could market me to a larger and more expansive audience. It was about that time that I heard that Vickie Stringer was starting a marketing and PR firm. I talked with her and told her that I was interested in having her firm represent me. During our first meeting, she said, "I know you are a very gifted speaker Tei, but it would be so much easier to market you if you had a book." My initial thought was, "I know a lot of speakers who are very successful and they don't have a book." But rather than give voice to my negativity, I sat down and tried to construct an outline for what would become this book.

I don't believe that the information contained in this book is revolutionary or revelatory. Many of the concepts have been expressed by others, but this book simply reflects my own personal thoughts about life, love, struggle, passion, patience, self-love, self-esteem, self-loathing, risk-taking, peer pressure and triumph over adversity.

Each chapter is short because it is meant to capture and engage the attention of young readers, who have little appreciation for things that drag on and on.

Though I had a youth audience in mind as I wrote, it is my hope that the content will be equally applicable to adults as well. I want people to be clear that many of the sensitive things I talk about are told only for the benefit of those who are going through tough times. I want them to know that they can survive the rough times and thrive in better times. When I see the statistics for teen suicide, my heart breaks because for some odd reason, no one is telling these young people that whatever they are going through will pass. It is temporary, but suicide is final.

One of the things that distinguishes this book from my speaking is that I am able to talk about my belief system in the book. Because I am often in public schools or other government sponsored events, I rarely have the opportunity to share my belief in God with students that I meet when I am speaking. So, though I believe that through my speaking God gives me messages that are life affirming and sustaining to share, the depth and profundity are diminished. This is because I believe that the greatest message that I can share with young and old alike is that God loves and cares for you. He wants to heal the parts of your soul that are hurting and replace them with joy that you cannot imagine. If you don't comprehend anything else in the pages to come, I hope that you comprehend that.

I know that there will be naysayers and people who will be critical of this book. But, I didn't take months of my life to appease them. I wrote this book for young people who are struggling every day on the front lines of failing schools, dangerous communities and dysfunctional families. The young people that I meet come from all walks of life. They are urban, suburban, rural; from many ethnicities, religions, cultures and socio-economic backgrounds. It has been in the last five years, through my speaking, that I have come to realize how much youth have in common. Many people believe that economic privilege alone is enough to safeguard some youth from the adversities of growing up. But, I can tell you that kids in the 'burbs struggle to find their place in the world as much as kids in the 'hood. Low self-esteem knows no financial boundaries and bullies come in all shapes, sizes and races. People abuse children from across the spectrum and most teens struggle to assert their independence. Given all of this, it should come as no surprise that kids across the globe have issues in common that cross their differences. This book is for them.

When people ask what made me want to work with teens, I always have to explain that working with youth was not a part of my original plan. However, thanks to the opportunity I was given to work with a program called Teen Institute (TI), I got to experience the possibilities of all youth. I will forever be grateful to TI, the oldest prevention program in the nation, for trusting me with our most precious natural resource, our youth. Ohio Teen Institute taught me how to work with young people effectively. I owe them for my career, because everything before then was just a collection of jobs. TI is the main reason I have a speaking career and it is my speaking that informed this book, so to the Ohio Teen Institute, I say, "You Rock!"

During the past year, I have been very fortunate to have many people to support my vision and to encourage me to continue writing - even when I had writer's block for four months. Only a few people doubted that I would complete this book. Most were sure that I would persevere and "practice patience." My three biggest cheerleaders in this process were Vickie Stringer, Kimberly Brant and my editor, Mia McPherson. Vickie continued to push me to write, even when I was resistant. She told me that she believed in me and in this book. She was in the process of writing her second novel and yet, she had time to give confidence to me. Kimberly Brant is the one adult that read my book, chapter by chapter, and gave me feedback. Her task was to inform me if the content was intelligible, readable and interesting. It was such a wonderful experience to have someone, whose opinion matters to me being my cheerleader. Mia, who was assigned to be my editor, was patient, thorough, supportive, longsuffering and the most positive person I know. She gave great editorial notes and worked hard to assure me that I was on the right track and that I would finish.

All three of these beautiful ladies are the reason that this short book has come to be.

Since I am not a writer, I hope that you know that this book really is a labor of my love for those who might read and be inspired by the words contained therein. Grace and Peace to you all!

CHAPTER 1

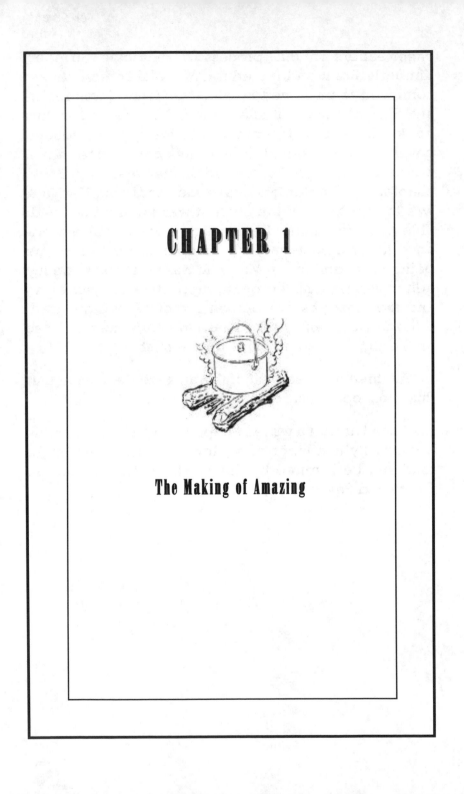

The Making of Amazing

"With confidence you can reach truly amazing heights; without confidence, even the simplest accomplishments are beyond your grasp." - Anonymous

Now I don't know about you, but as a young child, I often found myself alone, daydreaming and fantasizing in a world of my own. I fancied television characters as role models, and like most children mimicked the stunts, tricks and gimmicks practiced by my favorite characters. Of course to a child who is four or five, the warning "don't try this at home" served more as an invitation than a deterrent.

One of my favorite television personas was an illusionist known as "The Great Houdini." He was the master of illusion and would often perform tricks that left me spellbound. Once, I recall him being submerged in a tank of water with his hands and feet bound by handcuffs. Another time, I remember him being locked in a coffin (this one was not as intriguing because I am afraid of coffins and am claustrophobic) wherein he was tied up, the coffin was chained shut, enclosed in hay that was set afire. He escaped without being consumed by the flames. As he would come forth from each stunt, the announcer would say, "Ladies and Gentlemen, The Great Houdini." The crowd would erupt with thunderous applause at what seemed to be a wondrous feat.

Another time, I remember the announcer introducing him as "The Great Houdini, able to accomplish death defying feats." At five, I was not sure what a "death-defying feat" was, but I was sure it was something spectacular because of the inflection and anticipation in the voice of the announcer. It was then that I decided that I too wanted to be someone "great" who could "accomplish death-defying feats." So, I set about my life finding ways to be great, or in my case, "Amazing."

One day, at five, while playing alone in my basement, I mounted a stool that was about four feet high. Once atop the stool, I used one of my jump ropes to tie my feet together. Then, I removed the second rope from around my neck, placed my hands behind my back and commenced to tying them together. Suddenly a voice echoed in my head. The tiny, whispery voice said, at a very low decibel, "I'm The Amazing Tei Street." With every passing second, the voice grew louder. "I'm The Amazing Tei Street. I'm The Amazing Tei Street." Finally, with the voice so loud that it drowned out my thoughts, I began to wriggle loose from the ropes. Just as the ropes were about to loosen totally, I fell face forward from the stool. I broke my fall with my shoulder. The thud on the hard floor was overshadowed by the sound of a breaking bone. After using the side of my body that was not in severe pain, I freed myself from the ropes. I slowly limped up the stairs, trying to find a way to explain this whole sordid mess to my mother. This might not seem like a big deal to most people, but typical black mothers are generally not very understanding about crazy stunts such as this. So, when I finally reached my mother with my right arm dangling and tears of agony streaming down my face, she asked, "What happened, baby?" At the sound of her care and concern, I began to weep uncontrollably as I responded with the most sincerity I could muster, in light of what I was about to do. "I fell down the stairs." Immediately, she, like any concerned mother, scooped me up, put me in the car and rushed me to the emergency room. For the first time in my life, the lie worked. I must say that as the doctors were putting the half body cast on because I had broken my collar bone, I felt a little guilty. But, the guilt did not last long as I thought of how cool my kindergarten friends would think I was when they got to see and sign my cast. When I finally returned to school, I had a terrific time taking off my shirt, like an exhibitionist, for anyone and everyone to see my cast. Thinking back, it really was a horrific experience because in kindergarten, everyone who could write did not do it very well, nor did they do it with much speed. So one kid could use up my whole recess trying to sign his or her name. For the next six weeks, I could not play team games at school, write my assignments or play with my Barbie. Now I didn't mind missing out on the first two, but by the end of the six weeks, I was longing to "get my Barbie on," because playing with Barbie, Ken and the crew was my passion. Since there wasn't much to do, I spent much of my recuperation time contemplating other ways to achieve my goal of reaching my best and becoming "The Amazing

Tei Street." But for some odd reason, the little voice in my head had gone mute.

Though the voice was now non-existent, the actions continued as I dreamed of the day that I too would "accomplish death-defying feats" like my TV hero. Over the next few years, my mother decided that I should not have idle time on my hands, so she enrolled me in dance classes, girl scouts and my personal favorite, swimming lessons. I took to the water like a fish. I not only enjoyed swimming, but I became quite proficient at it. Eventually, I entered competitive swimming. Something inside made me want to be involved in anything that was competitive (which might explain why I hated dance). I had a swimming instructor named Laurie who would give rewards for the person in our swim class who could hold his or her breath the longest. I practiced every opportunity I got, in and out of the water. Finally, on the day of the big competition I discovered that I could hold my breath for two and a half minutes (or so they said). I was very excited about this, because it was all a part of my grand plan to execute my next great stunt.

That summer, just before my 9th birthday, is one I will always remember. My family and I were scheduled to go to New Jersey for a family reunion. This would be my big debut as I could show off my new skills for an audience. It didn't matter that my audience was comprised of my cousins, most of whom were nine or ten like me.

On the Saturday of the reunion, my cousins and I were all engaged in swimming. I went to the deep end of the pool. I had my cousins tie my hands behind my back with a plastic jump rope and tie my feet together with the second rope. I gave them very explicit instructions. I said, "If I am not up in three minutes, go get help because I am drowning." This was my first mistake. We were all swimming and no one had a watch. But did any of us note this? Absolutely not! So, just before I jumped into the deep end of the pool, I told my cousins my secret. I said, "I'm The Amazing Tei Street, I can accomplish death-defying feats."

They all said, "Whatever, just jump."

So, I said in my most confident voice, "I'm The Amazing Tei Street."

I leaped into the water and sunk to the bottom. (If someone wanted to kill me, they could dump me in any body of water and be assured that I would never float back to the top. Nothing about me floats.) As I was on the bottom of the pool struggling to get loose, I was humming, "M'm the Ammmmzng hmm Shhhh" (I'm The Amazing Tei Street).

After a while of not being able to free my self from the ropes I could tell that I had been submerged for a while, because my oxygen supply was diminishing. I could hear my cousins above asking such probing questions as, "Do you think she's dead?" and, "Is it time for dinner yet?" and, "Has it been three minutes yet?" I was particularly interested in the fact that someone was concerned about time, since I felt like I was dying. But to the all important question, my cousin, who was not the brightest bulb on the tree replied, "I don't think it's been three minutes. I think it has only been about 30 seconds." Normally, none of my cousins would have listened to anything he had to say, but they picked today of all days to allow him to be the expert. Thank God one of my older cousins came over and realized that I was in trouble and called for my uncle who was a lifeguard. He pulled me out of the water, still in my ropes. As I lay faking unconsciousness, I could hear my mother's voice. I was petrified to open my eyes and face my mom. After a while, I opened one eye and like any good mother, she was looking at me with great concern. Finally, I opened both eyes. Once she realized I was fine, she asked, "What in the world were you thinking?" I had finally mustered the courage to share my secret with the one person that I thought would encourage my dreams.

I looked at her with loving eyes and revealed the secret that I had held unto myself for the past 6 years and said, "Mom...I'm The Amazing Tei Street."

She did what so many parents do unintentionally; she crushed my dream and simultaneously my belief that the "Amazing" existed in me. She looked down at me lying on the concrete and replied, "You're the amazingly stupid Tei Street. Don't you know you could have drowned?" The lesson for me was, never tell your secrets to other people. When I got older, I buffered myself from people "hatin" on my dreams by keeping my goals and destinations to myself. African American activist/orator Reverend Jessie Jackson quotes, "If you don't want people to rain on your parade, don't tell them what street you are coming down." Those became my words to live by regarding my secret.

Once again, one of my stunts was a bust. But fear not, there are plenty more feats to accomplish. Before it's all over, "The Amazing Tei Street" will make several more appearances.

These are just two stories of my childhood quest to find the greatness within me. I'll let you in on a little secret early. I did finally reach "Amazing", but it was not through antics and stunts. The journey to becoming "The Amazing Tei Street" was accomplished with hard work and commitment to never giving up. It was achieved with the aid of many wonderful people who mentored me and passed along sage wisdom. It is that wisdom that I want to share with you in the following chapters. To become "Amazing" I had to learn and practice the steps to becoming a P.L.A.Y.A. (Person Living at Your Apex). If you are ready to become "Amazing," climb the steps with me.

CHAPTER 2

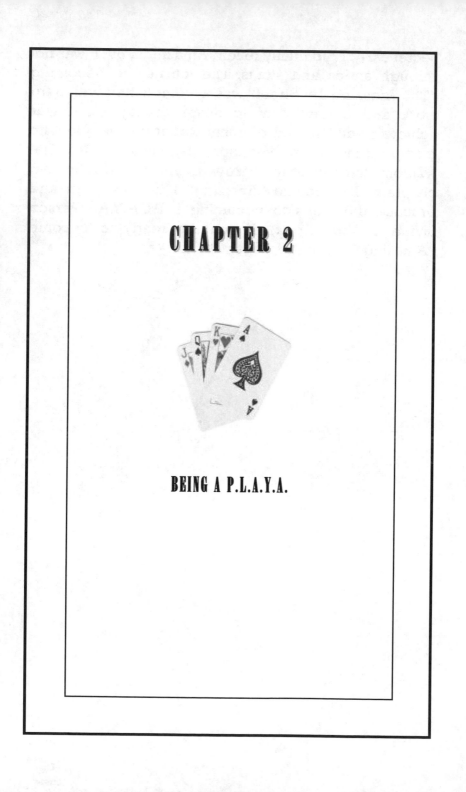

BEING A P.L.A.Y.A.

"I'm not a PLAYA, I just crush a lot."- Big Pun

In the contemporary vernacular, being a PLAYA generally refers to someone who has multiple dates, love interests or sexual partners - all of whom know nothing of the existence of the others. Further, young people in particular receive many "props" for being good in the practice of deception and validating their status as a PLAYA. Often, their peers voice their respect and admiration for PLAYAS by slapping high fives, winking or other non-verbal gestures. Sometimes however, they use such phrases as, "Go on PLAYA, handle yours," or "I ain't mad at cha' PLAYA." Whether verbal or non-verbal, the message is clear - being a PLAYA is optimal.

Well, I believe that in this era of STDs including

HIV/AIDS, to be that kind of PLAYA makes you a fool and quite possibly a dead fool. That is why I want to reclaim the term and use it as an acronym. So today, I assert that P.L.A.Y.A. stands for Person Living At Your Apex. An apex is the highest point. If we are talking about a mountain, the apex is the top of the mountain. If we are talking about a house, the roof or sometimes the chimney is the apex. When we are talking about human beings, an apex is your peak, your summit, your personal best or the top of your game. Now the apex looks different for each person, because you are the only person who can define and determine your personal best. For example, one of the ways that I knew I had reached my apex was when I started speaking and young people told me that my words had a profound impact on their lives. This was my apex because I had defined my personal best as having the opportunity to impact the lives of youth.

Now there is a significant difference between reaching your apex and living at your apex. To simply reach your goal is not the most difficult task. Don't get me wrong, reaching the goal requires diligence, perseverance and mad work. But if you think getting there is hard work, dig your heels in because living at your apex makes getting to it seem like a cake walk.

Don't let the warning of hard work dissuade you from going for your personal apex. In the next few chapters, I want to give you five steps to follow for reaching your apex and becoming a P.L.A.Y.A. The steps are self-explanatory, but they will require you to move beyond your comfort zone and trust that you can conquer your fears, doubts, self-loathing, low self-esteem, historical mistakes, fear of failure, fear of success and all of the other negative inhibitors that have kept you from getting to and living at your personal best; your apex.

It is appropriate to let you know here that my book is filled with some practical knowledge based on my own experiences. It is also filled with spiritual insight that I have gained from my personal walk with God. Just so there is no confusion, I want you, the reader, to know up front that I practice Christianity as my faith, thus much of my sharing is rooted in my Christian beliefs. It is not a prescription for anyone else's life, but certainly one perspective that is offered for your consideration.

CHAPTER 3

LOVE YOURSELF UNCONDITIONALLY
AND WITHOUT APOLOGY

"Who cares what they say? People are going to talk anyway. It's not how you look; it's how you feeeeeel on the inside." - Dorothy Love'll

If you are ever going to reach your best you must first look at the things that have been road blocks to your success in the past. I think that most of us begin the process of failure during childhood. Very early we learn from a variety of people that who we are is not OK. Most people never intend to scar us for life, but sometimes mere words are enough to cause us to hate ourselves. I still remember the terms used to describe me as a child, especially by my peers - Chiquita Banana, Inch High Private Eye and Ching Chong. I learned to hate myself each time my mother took me to the doctor and he asked, "What are you feeding her? You need to monitor what she is eating or she is going to be a real porker." I learned to hate myself each time someone said I was too short and that my nose took up half of my face. I learned to hate myself.

With all the years of learning to hate myself, it has and continues to be a daily walk to move beyond others' concepts of me. But I can tell you today that one of the reasons I live at my apex and am amazing is because first and foremost, I learned to love me unconditionally and without apology.

Sometimes when I talk about self-love, others attach labels to me such as conceited, narcissistic, (in Greek mythology, Narcissus looked in a mirror and fell in love with an image of himself) or arrogant. This is a good time to interject the distinction between arrogance and confidence. Arrogance is the overstatement of one's own self-importance, but confidence is the accurate assessment of one's own self-worth. You will soon learn that I am full of confidence. I am confident that I am worth self-love.

The only way to truly love yourself unconditionally is to have a relationship with the one who loved you unconditionally, first and best. My pilgrimage toward unconditional love ended when I discovered that the God who created the universe loved me first and best. He loved me enough to forgive and forget all of the things I had done in my past that made me feel unlovable. One day, I heard a young person tell me that she did not like herself because, "I think I am so ugly." At that very moment, I shared with her a thought that popped into my head. I told her, "Sweetie, God made you and me in his image, so if you say you are ugly, it's the same as saying, 'God, you sho' is ugly.' Now I don't know about you, but I am not going to be the one to tell God he is ugly." She and I both laughed, but it was in that moment that I realized that I was worthy of self-love because God must have thought a lot of man to create us in his image.

It never ceases to amaze me that millions of young people walk around the world in a cloud of self-doubt, self-mutilation, low self-esteem and self-loathing. My word to you is that you will find that there are those in your life who seek to destroy you, and the first step to destroying a person is assisting in destroying his or her self-concept. Don't give in to the BIG LIE that you are not the absolute best at any stage or state of your life. Believe the hype that you create in your head which says, "I am all that and then some."

I can tell you from personal experience that the road to self-love is a long, protracted one, filled with speed bumps and pot holes. But, I can also share that those who endure the journey toward self-love will find a reward of immeasurable proportion at the end of the road. There was a time in my life when I internalized all of the negative things I heard about myself. I believed that I was too short, too fat, too ugly, too dumb and too poor to ever amount to anything. Once outside influences succeeded (collectively, not individually) in convincing me that what I looked like would determine what I acted like, they had in essence taken the reigns of my destiny. I began to act out in school as a way of asserting that I was somebody. I made extremely poor choices that landed me in institutions for juvenile delinquents for most of my adolescence. It was in the institutions that I learned that not only was I ugly, but I had no real value to the world. It was at that time that I began to become physically abusive to myself, and I allowed others to abuse me.

With each assault on my mental, emotional and physical person, I learned to hate myself just a little bit more. In retrospect, I think that the lowest point in my life came when I was savagely raped by seven young people who were incarcerated with me. During my attack, they cut my hair and blacked both of my eyes. They laughed at the sight of me lying on the floor in a pool of my own blood, mangled as they said, "UGLY!" That day, I decided in my head and in my heart that if I was going to be ugly, I would act ugly. There began several years of truly self-destructive behavior and it all related back to the concept that I was ugly and unworthy of self-love or the love of anyone else.

For the young people reading this book, I know the internal battle you are fighting for self-love. I want to encourage you to look beyond the superficial by which we are all judged to find those things that make you uniquely you. Search within to find the things that you love about yourself regardless of how you look. Eventually, our looks will fade anyway, so it is important that we not base all of our self perspective on it. Christian poet Dorothy Love'll reminds us that it is that which we possess on the inside that is the truest sense of who we really are. In a poem, she asks, "Who cares what they say? People are going to talk anyway. It's not how you look. It's how you feeeeeeel on the inside."

I know this seems more easily said than done. But I will share a personal secret with you. When I wake up each morning, I have to make a choice to see me the way that God sees me. I have to choose to see myself as a beautiful woman, who, despite the fact that I am short and overweight, is still a representative of American beauty. I am fully aware that society says that being tall, thin and white is the ideal model of beauty. Thus, I must do double-duty in participating in self-loving rituals, because I have to compensate for not being the ideal height, the ideal weight and the ideal color. So, every morning, when I rise, I give thanks to God for allowing me to see another day. Then I go to my full length mirror to take a gander at my beauty.

If you decide to practice this ritual, you should know that it is important to do it first thing in the morning before you have done any of your pampering rituals. My philosophy is that if you can love yourself first thing in the morning, you can truly love yourself all day long. Picture how you look, smell and feel first thing in the morning. If you are like me, your hair is suffering from bed head, your breath is so "stanky" that it is forming its own path to the bathroom for you, your body is odiferous, your eyes are crusted shut, and slobber is pasted to the side of your face. Loving you at your earliest stage of the day means you can surely love yourself once you are showered, teeth are brushed, make-up applied, deodorant is on and hair is combed. In this state, I am loving me and not a façade.

When I look in the mirror and I see myself, I look with eyes of love. I say to myself, "Tei, Tei, Tei, Tei, Tei… you're short, your acne is off the hook and you are 'sho nuff' voluptuous, but girl, you are 'FOINE!'" I prefer the word voluptuous to the word fat. When someone asks me if I am gaining weight, I say, "No, I'm practicing voluptuosity. They say practice makes perfect, so it feels good to be on the verge of perfection."

This is not a recipe for loving yourself, but it is a wonderful ritual to help you get through each day, one day at a time. The real recipe comes from knowing that God loves you and that when he looks at you, he sees a creation of beauty and that no physical beauty can compensate for an ugly personality, just as no physical blemishes can mask a truly beautiful soul and spirit. For real beauty comes from within and emanates outward. So, the real secret for self love is finding the soul of beauty inside and polishing it to perfection and then sharing it with the world around you. One thing is sure, once you share it with a world wherein people are starving for love, you will indeed be a beacon of light. So, if you really want to be a PLAYA, you are well on your way when you learn to love yourself unconditionally and without apology.

CHAPTER 4

DRIVE YOUR OWN CAR

"No one is good enough, wise enough or cares enough, for you to turn over to them your future and your destiny." - Dr. Benjamin Mays

I am often asked if I could relive any era of my life, what era would I choose? I always respond by saying that I would definitely re-live my college years for they were the best years of my life. It was during those years that I came into my own as an African American, a woman and a leader. It was during this time that I learned to make decisions for myself that were truly in my best interest. College helped me to walk out of the shadows of my friends to frame my own thoughts. I no longer relied on the opinions of others to formulate my opinions. Yeah, this was by far the best era of my life. But by the same token, the era of my life that I would never want to re-live is middle school.

Back in the day, there was no middle school. There

was only elementary, junior high and senior high school. Elementary school went to 6th grade, junior high was 7th – 9th grade and high school was 10th -12th grade.

I moved to Ohio the summer before 4th grade and went to the neighborhood elementary school for 4th, 5th and 6th grades. I was so excited to contemplate the beginning of junior high. I looked forward to joining most of my classmates at our neighborhood junior high school. But, to my chagrin, my parents had other plans for me. One month before I was to begin 7th grade, my Mom informed me that I had been accepted to a school that was a part of a program called the Columbus Plan, and that I would be going to another junior high school. She then told me that I would be one of the few African American students. I told her that I really wanted to go to school with the rest of my friends. She told me that she had done her research and was convinced that this other school offered better academics. Call me crazy, but better academics are not exactly at the top of the list for 11-year-old kids. I just wanted to go to school with my friends, not have to make all new friends and just hang out having the time of my life. But that was not to be my fate. In September, I entered Yorktown Junior High School.

My first memory of my first day of 7th grade was the bus ride to school. We had to catch a bus at what seemed to be an ungodly hour, because all of the students who went to Yorktown, Sherwood or Johnson Park rode our bus and we had to make what seemed like 150 stops to pick up all of the students going to those three schools. When we finally reached Yorktown, I was so shocked that it took about 10 minutes for me to see the first African American student who was not me. I went to my homeroom and was deeply depressed to see only two other black students, besides me. Needless to say, we all sat in the same section. Soon, all of the white students were staring at us. The "three black stooges" were visibly uncomfortable, but we did our best not to let our classmates see us sweat. During the first few weeks of school, our classmates would not talk to us. They just continued the staring. We all looked forward to lunch because it was during that time that we had the support of the two black students who were in 8th grade and the one who was in 9th grade. I thought that six was forever to be my favorite number. (Oh yeah, there were three other black students, but they insisted they were not black; they were just human.)

It was in this group of six that I found solace and comfort from the plethora of insults that were constantly murmured in my direction. I spent the majority of that year working twice as hard to prove that I was as good as the white students. I was considered a "very bright" student, but teachers made it clear that they saw me as an anomaly. I remember on several occasions being the object of ridicule, not just from my peers, but from my teachers. When I tried to express my concerns to my mother, she just told me that I needed to toughen up because this was a good school wherein I could get a good education. Although I knew she was right, I did not care because to a 7th grade student, social interaction is number one on the priority scale and there was little positive interaction in what seemed and felt like hell!

I survived 7th grade without too much emotional damage, but I knew that one more year in this pressure cooker would surely push me over the edge. Nevertheless, my mother was determined to make me return to that same school.

I spent that summer trying to come up with good reasons why another school would be optimal. To my chagrin, when September finally came, it was back to Yorktown I went. The first thing I noticed when I got on the bus that morning was how many more new black students there were than the year before. I was so excited at the thought of having a larger cadre of people to "kick it" with who actually looked like me.

Well, 8th grade was off to a great start. Lots of cute guys were among the new groups of African Americans who came to our school. But the most exciting thing to happen was when someone with whom I had gone to elementary school came to Yorktown. For the purpose of protecting her reputation, I will call her Eva. Our mothers knew each other and we had been a part of the same clique in elementary school and had always gotten along. I spent much of the first month of school helping her to get acclimated. I was in heaven, especially in comparison to the alienation I felt the previous year. That was the year I had proposed in my heart to really excel academically by living up to my potential. My intelligence did not go unnoticed by my teachers or my peers. Little did I know that being bright would become the noose around my neck.

When we were in our second month of school, my friend Eva teamed up with the school bully and went on a reign of social terror. Soon I learned that I was one target of their mean, malicious, hateful campaigns of discredit. They taunted, teased and threatened. It didn't matter how much I tried to get around the behavior, it was only when I defended myself that they slowed their roll. One day, I was walking to my locker before homeroom. One of the bullies followed me down the hallway and started to call me names. For the few weeks leading up to this encounter, I had done my very best to ignore them as my mother had always instructed me. I continued to walk down the hall, passing by the art teacher.

My friend, who was brave enough to still be my friend, was walking beside me. She said, "You have taken this s—— long enough. Turn around and kick her butt." Though she was pumping me up, I tried really hard to ignore her because I knew that if I had a fight I would be suspended. I had never been suspended and I was sure that I did not want to face my mother if I got suspended. So, when I reached my locker, I opened it and ignored the bully and her pack. Her taunting got louder and closer until she was upon me. I closed my locker and walked away. She came up behind me and hit me in the back of the head. I was going to walk to my art teacher, but my "friend" said, "If you walk away, you are a punk." I immediately turned around and chose poorly to swing on the bully. The fight commenced. When it was all over, she had a busted lip and a bloody nose.

When they took me to the office I was so nervous because I had never been there for misbehavior. The principal finally called me and the bully in separately. She informed me that I was being suspended for 3 days. She called my mother, who asked if I was OK. The principal informed her that I was fine, but my opponent did not fare as well. My mom asked if I started the alter-cation. The principal indicated that the art teacher reported that I did not start the fight, but told my moth-er that Columbus Public Schools' policy dictated that both parties of a fight were to be suspended.

When my mother came to pick me up I was afraid to

face her, but she was remarkably calm. She said that she respected the fact that I had tried to prevent the fight, but was glad that I did not let someone beat me up without defending myself. She used the age old cliché, "You better not start a fight, but you better end it." Today, I will reveal a secret to you. I had participated in many fights in my neighborhood, but I did not want to fight that bully that day. And I can honestly say that I would not have fought her if my "friend" had not insinuated that I would be a "punk" if I did not fight her. That was the beginning of my adolescent battle with negative peer pressure. It was the first of many battles I would lose against this seemingly unconquerable beast.

After my suspension, I went back to school and my peers seemed to have developed a new respect for me. I liked the way it felt to no longer be a victim. Soon, I found myself on a pathway of negative choices, all in an effort to please and impress my peers. That year alone, I would be suspended a total of 11 times. My parents didn't know what to do with me. They tried everything from discipline to counseling, but nothing seemed to work. I hated myself, but I thought I was masking the self-hatred with verbose, negative, rowdy, disrespectful, lewd and obnoxious behavior. Though I wanted to get back on the right track and have my parents respect and trust me again, the draw to have my peers give me "props" for my behavior outweighed even my desire to please my parents, or for that matter, to please God.

I spent the summer on punishment and cut off from the outside world. I went back to school in the fall, but nothing had changed for me. In fact, my behavior was worse. I was expelled from Yorktown for throwing and landing a knockout punch at a teacher. I did it to the cheer of my peers. Once again, they, not I, were in control of my life. That particular event catapulted me from the minor leagues of juvenile delinquency to the majors. This time, I graduated from suspension to expulsion and from a school/family matter to a judicial matter. I did my first stint in the juvenile detention center. When I went to court, the judge ordered me to stay out of trouble at my new school, to attend weekly counseling sessions and to report weekly to a probation officer. My family was so embarrassed, but they stood by me. My parents paid for my attorney and for the counseling mandated by the courts.

Even the courts were not more powerful than peer pressure. I continued on a negative path for the next four years. Eventually, the courts took custody from my parents and placed me in the custody of the state. Even locked up, I continually made bad choices that seemingly impressed those locked up with me. My bad choices finally landed me locked up away from everything familiar and known to me and woefully behind in school. And still, I made bad choices.

Looking back, I realized that by allowing my peers, friends, class/cellmates to influence my decision-making skills, I was allowing them to drive the most valuable car I would ever own. This car wasn't a Benz, Beemer, Jag, Honda or an SUV. The car they were driving was called my life.

When my sister got her first car at 16, my mother told her that none of her friends were insured to drive her car. She told her that if she allowed them to drive it and they had an accident, the insurance company would not pay to replace the car and she would be making payments on a car that was inoperable. I spent a lot of time with my sister and her friends and I was always impressed with the fact that no matter how many times her friends asked to drive her car, her answer was always the same. She would say, "I would like to, but I am the only person insured to drive it and if you wreck it, I am stuck without a car." She usually made good choices and even when she made the occasional bad choice, it certainly wasn't from the influence of her friends.

The lesson of driving your own car is one I want to share with everyone struggling to fit in by giving in to peer pressure. Your life is like my sister's car. You are the only person, other than God, who is licensed to drive your life. If you allow your friends to negatively influence you, you are giving them the keys to your most valuable asset; you. If you wreck your life by allowing others to convince you to do destructive things to yourself and your life, they are not the people who will suffer. You are the ultimate person who will be the wreckage when you allow others to drive your car. Dr. Benjamin Mays, who is the President Emeritus of Morehouse College in Atlanta, gave us sound advice. He said, and I concur, "No one is good enough, wise enough, or cares enough for you to turn over to them your future and your destiny." Each time I allowed my friends to get me to make poor choices, I put my future and my destiny in their hands instead of my own. I allowed them to drive my car and then when I crashed into a tree, I paid the consequences, not them. In fact, to this day, I barely remember most of their names, but for them and my poor choices, I was incarcerated in one way or another for almost 4 years. I missed all of my adolescence to poor choices.

So, when it is time to make choices like whether or

not to drink, do drugs, engage in sex outside of marriage and a host of other non-healthy choices, ask yourself, who do you want driving your car? If you drive it and you wreck it, you can't blame anyone but you. If you allow your friends to drive your life car and they help you wreck it, you will have to live with the consequences. I want to encourage you to use my life as an example of what not to do. Be stronger than I was. Love yourself, because people with high self-esteem are less susceptible to negative peer pressure. In a nutshell, with God at the helm, DRIVE YOUR OWN CAR!!!

CHAPTER 5

FACE YOUR FEARS

"He who fears something gives it power over him." –Moorish Proverb

It is said that the number one fear of Americans is public speaking, with death sprinting along as a close second. Having worked with groups of young people to teach basic public speaking skills, I am inclined to believe that more Americans fear public speaking than death. I have witnessed people turn red, turn pale, throw up, battle diarrhea, hemorrhage from the nose and faint at the thought of having to address even a small group of people.

Most, if not all of us, are afraid of something. Some people are afraid of mice, snakes (I have not faced, nor conquered this one), spiders, dying, flying or the ever-popular heights, clowns and feet. As a child, though I loved the water, I was afraid of flying and heights. As much as I loved vacations, I dreaded the ones that required us to fly. I was so afraid of the take off and the landing. In addition to motion sickness, I often experienced what I called the roller coaster effect on my stomach. As the plane would be rising, my stomach would be in my knees. The same was true for the landing. I would be given something to make me sleep. I guess my mom learned early that if anyone was to have peace on the plane, I would need to be knocked out. Personally, I preferred the trips on which we drove. As long as I was by a window that I could crack open from time to time, my motion sickness was controllable in a car. In hindsight, I think my fear of heights was connected to my fear of flying. I would always imagine the plane falling from the sky and dying on impact with the ground. Now that I think of it, another fear that I had was a fear of dying. So, all three fears were inextricably linked and each time I was to fly I had to face all three.

Facing one fear is difficult enough for an adult, so imagine the overwhelming feeling that plagued my mind as a child.

The problem with my fear of flying, heights and dying was the problem with all fears that we as humans face. As I reached adulthood, especially during my college years, I wanted to see the world with my friends. Suddenly, I realized that my fears were prohibiting me from reaching my dreams and my goal of seeing different parts of America and the world. I had a college roommate who loved to travel, and we always went on vacation during breaks between quarters. At first, it was not problematic because we mostly traveled to the East Coast and to the South. Eventually, however, we wanted to visit the West Coast and London and I knew that it would require me to fly. The very thought of it made me physically and psychologically ill. My fear of flying really shocked my roommate because she was used to me having an adventurous nature. Some of the adventures we experienced included scuba diving and sailing on a trip to Cape Cod, renting and riding motorcycles, whale watching, mopeding down a rocky path in North Carolina, riding the subways in New York (just kidding NY), and taking her (a white female) to Harlem. But nonetheless, I would not fly.

I remember watching TV one day and seeing people skydive. It looked like the most freeing experience in the world. I remember longing to be floating through the air like that. I told my roommate (as I had told others over the years) that someday, I wanted to go parachuting. When I mentioned it to my other friends, they said, "Girl, black people do not jump out of airplanes."

And though I was really afraid, the thought of it stimulated me and the idea resonated in the back of my mind for a long time to come.

One day I was driving to Cincinnati from Dayton with my boyfriend, my friend Dawn and her boyfriend. We were going to window shop and see a play.

My boyfriend was on leave from the Army and he liked taking me to the theatre when he was home because I loved it so, and as a college student I could not afford to go on my own. As we were driving, we passed a field and beside the road was a sign that read, "For $200 & a 2 hour class, you can take your initial jump TODAY!" The sign had a picture of someone skydiving. I was just talking out loud, but I said to my friends, "Someday, I going to jump out of a plane." My boyfriend called my bluff by saying, "Do it today, baby." I couldn't believe he put me on front street, so I gave him the look of death.

I said, "You know I'm a 'po' college student and I don't have $200." I thought that would appease him and my friends and get me off the hook.

But he piped in and said, "Baby, I have $200 and I'll pay for the class."

I cut him a cross eye and said between clinched teeth, "SHUTUP!"

At that very moment, my friend Dawn chimed in with, "I'll give you $50 if you jump today." Now $50 may not seem like a lot of money to most people, but when you are a poor college student, $50 is like $500. As a big girl, I have to admit that I had visions of cheeseburgers and pizzas dancing in my head. Still, $50 was not enough to risk my life, especially since I didn't know if my parents had a life insurance policy on me. So, I kept driving.

Then, Dawn's boyfriend said, "OK, I'll give you another $100 if you jump today." The thought of $150 put my car on auto pilot as it made an immediate U-turn.

When I got to the class, there were five other people taking the class in preparation for their first jump. Our instructor was a guy in his mid-30s named Paul. For the next two hours, Paul told us everything there was to know about sky diving. I have to admit that I was too nervous to focus on what he was saying to us. During the whole two hour session, my heart was beating a mile a minute and the beat was so loud that it drowned out the instructor's voice. However, I am a self-preservationist, so my ears naturally perked up at two parts of the lecture.

Paul said that when we pulled the rip cord and the parachute opened, it would "propel" us upward. This caught my attention because I am well-endowed in the chest area. So, anything that will propel me upward makes me a little nervous, because with the wrong movement, I could end up with black eyes. The other thing that Paul said that got my attention was, "Upon landing, tuck and roll." This caught my attention because like most big people, I cannot tuck and roll. I could shoot a 3 point jump shot all day long and still almost failed physical education class because I could not tuck and roll.

All I could think was, "Great, I'll survive the jump and then break my neck on the landing." Nonetheless, the class came to an end and it was time to get into our jumpsuit, strap into our harnesses and get on the plane. At this point, I stopped to say a long prayer and climbed aboard.

Once we were on the plane, we sat in the order in which we intended to jump. I was number four of six. There were three men and three women including me. I learned a few things about my jump mates during the class, because each was willing to share his and her life story. I was much too nervous to hear or care about most of what they were saying. When the first guy got up, he was so stereotypical. He was a typical jock and acted as though he was not afraid of anything. After Paul gave the group a pep talk and said he'd see us on the ground, this guy stood up. He moved confidently to the door, pulled down his goggles, gave a "thumbs up", took a deep breath and jumped. All I could think was, "WOW." Now, I have to tell you that I had proposed in my heart that if anyone decided that they were not going to jump, I was not going to jump either.

The next guy got up. Unlike the first guy, I could tell that he was very nervous. Of course, he did not want us to know that he was nervous, so he kept wiping his hands on his pants. Secretly, I was quietly praying, "Don't jump dude, don't jump dude." After about two minutes of working up his nerve, he moved closer to the door. I knew that I couldn't count on him to save me from jumping when I saw him pull his goggles down and say a quick prayer. He crossed himself and then jumped.

The only hope that I had was the older woman who was in front of me named Sarah. I remember her name because during the course of our two hour class, she told us her life history. Included in this history was the fact that she was 52 (at 22, 52 seemed old to me, but not anymore), her husband left her for a younger woman and her children were grown and off at college. She said this is what gave her the impetus to jump. When Sarah stood up, she moved toward the door very slowly. In fact, she walked like a baby with a full diaper. She was bent over about the shoulders. When she was close to the door, she looked at the instructor and said, "I don't know Paul."

He immediately moved to the role of chief motivator. He said, "You can do it Sarah."

Again, she said, "I don't know Paul."

Finally, Paul looked at her and said, "Sarah, what have you got to lose? Your husband left ya' and your kids are grown." I thought to myself "wow that's low." But it seemed to work for Sarah. I think perhaps it was the anger over being left that galled Sarah and became the catalyst for her courage. After that statement, she straightened up and confidently moved toward the door. As she pulled her goggles over her eyes, I could hear my mind chanting, "Don't do it Sarah, Don't do it Sarah, Don't do it Sarah." I knew that my chanting was in vain, because it was not long before she joined her predecessors in the clouds. It was finally my turn.

There was no way that I was going to be outdone by a 52 year old woman. Even though I was very nervous, I walked to the door with the coolest black woman pimping swagger I could manage. When I got to the door I held on for dear life, as my knees were shaking like California during an earthquake. At that moment, Paul tried to seize the moment to be a motivator, but his words were wasted on me. I learned very early how to tune out the voices of others to listen to my own inner voice. So, I gave him a nonverbal "talk to the hand" without the gesture. Just when I thought my nerves were going to force my lunch up, a calmness overcame me. Bet you can't guess what happened. ?

After all those years, I got a visit from a familiar voice from the past. Just when I thought she was gone, she showed up in time to save me and the day. Just as I was about to back out and go back to my seat, a little voice whispered in my head, "I'm The Amazing Tei Street." It had been so long since I had heard from her that it almost scared me. However, I quickly collected myself and allowed her to flow. She said, "I'm The Amazing Tei Street, I can accomplish death-defying feats." The voice got louder as Paul continued to babble in my ear. Suddenly, I lowered the goggles, tugged on the straps of my harness to be sure they were tight, said a prayer, open my mouth and said, "I'm the Amazing Tei STREEEEEEEEEEEEEEEEEEEEEEEEEETTTTTTTTT." I couldn't believe it, but I was floating through the clouds. It was the most freeing experience of my life.

This was a natural high that far surpassed any drug that you could try. All of a sudden, it occurred to me that I could try some things that I was not capable of doing on the ground. My first feat was a cartwheel, then a front flip and for the grand finale, a back flip. I was having the time of my life. Looking out made me know without a doubt that God existed.

I lost track of everything, including the fact that I was moving rapidly downward. I looked down and could see these little ants that I soon realized were people. It should not surprise you that I thought they were cheering and dancing, "Go Tei-Tei, Go Tei-Tei"(especially given my admitted confession that I am a bit egotistical). They were not cheering, they were shouting and gesturing, "Pull your chute!" I gathered my thoughts and pulled the rip cord on the chute. I suddenly realized that Paul had greatly mistaken the intensity of what was taking place. He told us that the chute would "propel" us upward. There was no propelling, there was an upward jerk that almost gave me whiplash. My heart was beating so hard that I thought I saw it coming through my jumpsuit. I thought to myself, "Oh great, I survived the jump, but will have a heart attack." Just when my heart was calming down, it was then time to focus on the fact that I had to tuck and roll in about one minute. I knew this was not to be.

I decided to spare myself the embarrassment and make up my own landing. It was not a pretty landing, but I survived. When I landed, the instructor on the ground came over to take off my chute. My friends were coming out to greet me. When they reached me, I am sure you know what I asked. Yep, "Where's my money?" As Dawn and her boyfriend were handing me my $150, they all were laughing uncontrollably. I was getting a little annoyed because I thought they were laughing at my landing. Dawn had tears streaming down her face. I said to them, "What? I just jumped out of an airplane. I'm The Amazing Tei Street." As they tried to collect themselves, Dawn pointed at my lower extremities. I looked down and I was soaking wet. I suddenly realized that as the chute went up, the "pee-pee" came down. I faced my fears head on, but I did it in wet pants.

Today, I make my living flying across the country speaking to young people. If I had not faced my fears, my movement would be restricted to the East Coast, Midwest and South. Could I really deny people in other parts of the US the opportunity to hear "The Amazing Tei Street"? If you don't face and confront your fears, they will stifle you and keep you from reaching your dreams and goals. The Bible teaches us that "God has not given us the spirit of fear." God in His infinite wisdom knew that fear was an inhibitor, not an enhancer of the human spirit. Face your fears and they become stepping stones towards your destiny and not stumbling blocks along your journey. Who knows, you might just have some awesome experiences along the way.

CHAPTER 6

BECOME A POSITIVE ROLE MODEL

"You Can't Teach What You Don't Know and You Can't Lead Where You Won't Go."
–Author Unknown

When I was ten years old, my parents became Born-Again Christians. The change in their lives meant a radical change in the lives of my siblings and me. Suddenly, the things that we had always done were now forbidden by their religion such as listening to secular music. I, of course, thought it was ludicrous and went about life defying anything associated with Christianity. Though I did not understand or like my parents' "new life," I respected them for their unyielding faith in God and to the principles they espoused. My mother was always sure to live the kind of life that she said she believed. She treated people with Christian love as ascribed by the Bible. She did not live a dual life. She practiced those things that she believed were a part of God's will for her life. Additionally, she taught us those same principles and though we did not always share her beliefs or practice them ourselves, it did not deter her from sharing her beliefs through her verbiage, but more importantly through her living. From her life I learned the importance of using our lives as an example for others. It is not enough however to say positive things. You must be willing to live positive lives.

Each of us has the unique opportunity to be a positive role model for someone else. In my own life, I try to be a positive role model for young people. There are lots of youth who look up to me and through my life example, I try to be a good role model for them. I have the awesome opportunity to talk with youth about making positive choices, such as saying no to drugs and alcohol, remaining sexually abstinent and choosing good friends. In my personal life, I have a firm commitment to living an alcohol, tobacco and drug free lifestyle. Additionally, as a Born-Again Christian, I reconstituted my body to God and as such, I practice sexual abstinence until marriage. Further, I surround myself with good people who also make good choices.

In my own life, I have been blessed with a plethora of good, positive role models that God placed in my path. As I have already told you, the person who had/has the most profound impact on my life is my mother, Theresa Street. Though we are estranged, I would be remiss if I didn't acknowledge her as one of the most dynamic, intelligent, awesome and righteous women to ever grace my life. Though she came from humble beginnings, she taught me that upward mobility is not about how much money one has, but about leaving the world a better place than when you entered it. She taught me the importance of legacy. Like her mother before her, she taught my sister, brother and I, that legacy was about teaching your children strength, courage endurance and pride in who you are and in what you achieve. My mother taught me that the world does not owe us anything and that we are not entitled to anything that we don't earn through blood, sweat and tears.

My sister Tanya taught me the importance of spending time with those coming behind you. As a teenager, she always found time to include me in her day-to-day activities. She never neglected me to hang out with her friends. Though I am seven years younger than she is, she took me on many outings with her friends. She was my advocate and the epitome of black beauty. Though I knew I would never be as beautiful inside or out as she, she certainly gave me something for which to strive. I am not sure if she ever knew how much I not only loved her, but admired her. When she was in high school, I remember that she was very popular and was never without a choice for dates. The thing I admired most is that she was popular with the guys, but never sacrificed her virginity to maintain her popularity. She understood well the lesson that no one wants what everyone else has had. In hindsight, I wish that I had followed her lead and maintained my virginity until marriage. She believed, (and still does) that sex outside of marriage was wrong and she lived that which she believed.

As an adult, she gained my respect by being a sensational mother and teacher. Though she has faced many challenges in both roles, she always finds the silver lining in every dark cloud. She is positive and productive in her home and work life. She never gives up and won't allow her children or the children in her class to give up. She is loyal, faithful and true as a person and as a friend. Those are traits I have learned to value and possess. So, obviously, I consider her one of my great role models.

Apart from my mother and my sister, the person whose life example has had the most profound impact on my life is Emery Hill. I wanted to be just like her. She was intelligent, witty, hard-working, beautiful, polished and a member of the most illustrious black women's organization in the world, Delta Sigma Theta Sorority, Inc. Emery was the epitome of class. I can honestly say that our relationship did not start off on a good note. In fact, it started off as rocky as any relationship could.

After spending several years in juvenile facilities across the state of Ohio, I was ill-equipped to face the challenge of being in a formal school setting. But there I was, enrolled in Mifflin High School as a 16-(almost 17) year-old freshman. I was essentially biding my time until I turned 18, because being enrolled in school was a requirement of my probation officer when he agreed to foster care placement in Columbus with my guardian angel, Robin McClendon Shoemaker.

Because it had been so long since I was in a formal school setting, I had forgotten all of the rules that went along with being in school, such as being quiet in classes. One day, I was in my English class, talking with my new friends. My teacher, who was feared by every student who was forced to take a class from her, was Emery S. Hill. She was a stickler for rules, order and discipline in her classroom. She was also committed to academic excellence for her students at all costs. Her reputation preceded her as a tough, no-nonsense teacher who was no stranger to failing students who did not excel. As I was talking during her lecture, Mrs. Hill said, "Ms. Street, be quiet." I politely rolled my eyes at her and commenced to finishing my conversation. (*It is important to note here that I had always struggled with authority figures, especially in schools and was not used to practicing deference to teachers.)

She was shocked by my lack of attention to her directive. She yelled, "I said be quiet and that's what I mean. If you say one more word, you are going to the office." In my mind, I was thinking, "Cool, if I get sent to the office, I will get suspended and get to go home, take a nap and watch TV."

I looked at her with sarcasm in my eyes and utter defiance in my voice and boldly said, "WORD!" I did not know that that one simple statement would change my entire life. She stood up and ordered me to go to stand in the hallway.

I replied, "You said I was going to the office."

She clinched her jaw and grinded her teeth and as her eyes seemed to disappear behind her lids, she snarled, "I changed my mind!!" I rose from my chair and walked to the door in what seemed like slow motion, in an effort to annoy her. As I was standing in the hallway waiting for her to emerge from the room, thoughts of my past flashed before my eyes. Suddenly I was filled with an arrogant boldness and was ready to face whatever she brought. After about 10 minutes, she came through the door, grabbed me by my collar and pushed me up against the lockers. For the first time in a long time, I was "Skurrrred."

As she tightened her grip, she looked me in my eyes and said, "Let me tell you something, little girl. If you let me, I'll be as good as gold to you, but if you cross me,

I'll be the biggest B—— you have ever encountered. Now you are going to go back in that class, sit down and shut-up. Do I make myself clear?" Shaking in my shoes, I nervously shook my head in the affirmative. I re-entered the class, sat down and did my work. From that day on, she committed herself to helping me to change my life. She required my absolute best and worked to make sure that I would graduate. When I would occasionally slip back into my old ways of behaving, my other teachers would not send me to the office, they would send me to see Emery. As much as I loved and respected her, I also feared her. After a few frightening visits to her office I soon decided that doing what I was supposed to do was so much easier. She enlisted the support of the drama teacher, Sally Kriska, who gave me a chance to shine on the stage. That gave me the incentive to remain suspension-free. The assistant principal, Mrs. Gene Harris (now Columbus Public School Superintendent, Dr. Gene Harris) lent her support by making sure that on those occasions when I needed chiding and correction, she was there to let me know that she would not accept anything but my best. With this circle of strong, positive role models, it should not be a secret to anyone that I was suddenly on a path to success. I am not sure if they know it, but I believe they collectively saved my life.

The next year, I got a fairy-god family. I spent my senior year of high school living with Terry, Christina and Zachary Shields. Though they were a white family, it was the first time since I left my own family that I felt like I had a real home and a real family. Christina was the music teacher at Mifflin and she learned that I was living a homeless existence. She and her wonderful husband and son invited me to live my senior year in their home. Suddenly, I had access to a part-time job, a car, food, clothing and a place where all of my friends could hang out. That year, the Shields made sure that all of my needs and most of my wants were met. I relaxed into this new situation and had one of the most wonderful years of my life. At the end of the year, they hosted a wonderful graduation reception to honor the fact that I was graduating from high school and entering college at The Ohio State University. It was a wonderful year and I am blessed that they still choose to be a part of my life, because good friends should last a lifetime.

As I entered The Ohio State University, I thought that my days of having awesome people in my path were surely over, because after all, I was grown. I didn't have a clue that I would still need positive people in my life to make sure that I stayed on path of destiny. But, I am so glad that God knew what I would need. Though I won't tell you all of their stories and how they impacted me, I have to tell you that at the appropriate times (when I needed the lessons they had to teach me at that time), more positive role models and mentors/friends showed up.

My mentors/friends at Ohio State included Cynthia Zachary-Smith, Ruth Sallee Gresham, Dr. Joe Stranges, Pat Williams, Rebecca Parker, Rebecca Nelson, Mr. Willie Young and Linda Morrison. Their guidance helped me to navigate through the storms of a university that struggled with issues of race, gender and class. I am so grateful to them because after my high school mentors gave me my wings, my college mentors taught me how to flap those wings and soar above even that which I could imagine. They each excelled and accepted nothing less than my personal best as I faced adversity and challenges of being an African American woman in a predominantly white institution. I learned how to be strong, fight for that which I believed and how to be an advocate, warrior and ally for those who can't negotiate the world on their own terms. Though I did not know at that time that I would someday have the opportunity to work with young people, the lessons they taught me then were the lessons that would prepare me for what would be my destiny. I didn't know that when Willie Young told me that "not every flower blooms on the first day of spring," I would someday use that lesson to inspire teachers and parents not to give up on children who struggle. I didn't know that when Cynthia Zachary-Smith told me that "it is good to fight for other communities, but charity begins at home," that I would someday use that lesson to teach youth how to change their own communities. But, once again, God knew then who and what I needed in my life and made sure that positive role models continued to illuminate my pathways.

Even today, I have wonderful role models who inspire, uplift, motivate and correctly advise me. My best friends, Dr. Siri Briggs-Brown and Dr. Sakile Kai Camara continually challenge me to do what is right, even when I stubbornly want to sometimes choose wrong. They lovingly support me in my aspirations, but because they love me, they also "check" me when I am on a negative bent or headed down a path that is not in my own best interest.

My Spec, Dr. Dionne Blue, encourages me to reach for my dreams and makes sure that I don't use excuses for not succeeding. My Spec, Terina Matthews, reminds me daily that I am called of God and as such I have a responsibility to walk upright before God and my fellow humans. My Spec, Kimberly Brant, reminds me daily that I am not here for my own purpose, but rather to be an instrument for God's use.

My SANDS, Quiona Stephens, teaches me the importance of keeping God at the forefront of my life and my thoughts. She intercedes for me and encourages me to intercede for others. My SANDS, W. Shawna Gibbs, continually teaches me the importance of professional ethics and professional excellence. She is "THAT DEAL" and her example makes me want to be "that deal" too. My Soror, Regina R. Harper, taught me the importance of forgiveness both for the forgiver and for the forgiven.

My friend, Vickie Stringer, is a constant reminder that God is a Restorer and that your past is your history, but where God wants to take you is your destiny. My friend, Robyn Price, teaches me that faith is more than a profession, it is a lifestyle choice. My godson, Devin Price, has taught me that children don't have to come through you to be impacted by you. He re-ignited the spark in me when he thought I was lighting one in him. My friend and colleague, Heidi Yoakum, continually teaches me that all young people are "at promise" versus at risk. She taught me that doing good work is very important, but doing God's work is most important. The thousands of young people across this country who continually make good choices in the face of a world gone MAD are the real heroes of my life.

I am always amazed when young people are asked who their role models are and they begin to name a laundry list of famous entertainers, athletes and other stars. I guess my amazement comes from my realization that most of the young people who see stars as role models will never have the benefit of knowing those they idolize. Even if they do get to meet them, it will more than likely be a fleeting, chance meeting. Even this brief encounter will not afford them the time, investment or modeling necessary to make a significant impact. Therefore, it is incumbent upon each of to stand in the gap and step up to the plate to be a role model for a young person in each of our lives. They may never meet Shaquille O'Neal, Serena Williams, Mia Hamm, Shania Twain, P-Diddy, Nelly or any other famous person, but they can meet and know YOU!!! Imagine how good it would feel to have a young person say, "When I grow up, I want to be like you." Now, that's the stuff of which the American Dream is really made.

Essentially, there are many people who have mentored me and who continue to mentor me through the highlights and the pitfalls of life. The positive role modeling of others to me has laid the blueprint for me to be a positive role model for others.

BECOME A POSITIVE ROLE MODEL! This is your assignment, should you choose to accept it. If you do, you are in for a lifetime of relationships and a legacy of responsibility.

CHAPTER 7

"No Deposit, No Return"

PUT SOMETHING IN SO YOU CAN GET SOMETHING OUT". –Moorish Proverb

Once, when I was a graduate student, I went to a conference in Washington, D.C. At that time, we were paid only once per month and it was on the last working day of the month. It so happened that I was traveling to D.C. on the same day that we got paid. I was rushing and did not have time to deposit my paycheck before going to the airport. As someone who did not keep very good track of my bank account, I just assumed that I had some funds in my account and reasoned that when I arrived in D.C., I would simply go to the ATM machine in the airport.

When my plane arrived in D.C., I deplaned and proceeded directly to the ATM. I put my card in the machine and entered a withdrawal in the amount of

$60. It came back, with a "sorry for you" message. So, I lowered my aim and entered $40. This time the machine was like, "Yeah right." Finally, I tried the lowest denomination possible, $20. The machine spit back a piece of paper that said, "What part of sorry about your luck don't you get? You are as broke as a joke." It was at this point that panic set in. I realized I was in hot water because D.C. is a very expensive city.

Reluctantly, I sauntered over to the pay phone and made the dreaded collect call to my mother. I knew that if she were able, she would certainly not leave me stranded in D.C. However, I also knew that the money was sure to be accompanied by a lecture. As I stood sobbing uncontrollably while explaining the ATM catastrophe to my mom. When I was finished telling her what had just happened, she calmly asked, "Didn't you get paid today?"

Sniffling, I said, "Yes."

She said, "Then why don't you have any money?"

I said, "I didn't have time to go to the bank to deposit my check. I thought I would just get money out of the ATM when I got to Washington."

In her usual logical and rational tone, she said, "If you didn't put any money in the bank, what made you think you were going to be able to get any money out of the bank?" My mom did wire me the money I needed for the weekend, but that question would be one that resonated in my mind throughout the rest of my life.

The lesson that I learned that night in the Dulles Airport extended well beyond money and finances. From my mother's question came a life lesson that I carry with me to this day. That lesson is that the world does not owe you anything. You should not feel entitled to anything that you have not earned. Basically, a Disney movie from my childhood stated it best in the title, "No Deposit, No Return."

Often, we or our loved ones make excuses for us when we don't accomplish those things that we set out to accomplish. When one of the students in a program I run did not make the grades necessary to continue in good standing with my program, his mother came to meet with me. When I reiterated the conditions for continuation with the program, she began to make excuses for why her son was not making the grade. She said, "He tries so hard, but his teachers don't like him. When he comes to the program after school he doesn't think the tutor knows how to assist him with his work. I think the odds are stacked against him and no one will give him a chance to succeed." After listening to her litany, I pulled out his daily homework and behavior chart. When I showed her the number of days that he reported not having any homework, she was dumb-founded. She did not know what to say.

Further, when I showed her the number of times that he had been referred to the after-school director for refusing to do his work, she began to stutter. I said to her, "As long as you make excuses for your son, he will never step up to the plate to do what needs to be done to succeed in his quest to pass the 7th grade. But essentially, if he doesn't put anything into his academics, he won't get anything out."

A couple of years ago, I was complaining to my mom that what was once an expansive vocabulary for me was now dismal at best. She asked how often I read for pleasure and not for work. It took me a few minutes to realize that it had been some time since I had read for fun. She reminded me that my brain is a muscle and if I did not exercise it, it would not function at maximum capacity. I decided that day that I would begin to read something every day in a quest to keep my brain cells functioning properly.

Each day we have the wonderful occasion to learn something new, give something back and make our lives better. Note that the ownership for each of the above rests with us as individuals, not with others. We each have a responsibility to walk in life recognizing our accountability for building lives that we love. What each of us is capable of becoming is not always clear or evident. But, we can be sure that if we don't invest in our lives, our education, our homes, our country, our spirits, there will be no funds from which to withdraw those things necessary for healthy, productive lives. We can be like people who scream at the wind or we can work actively to put something into our lives, so that with good reason, we can expect to get something out. There is a good book that says, "Ye shall reap what you sow." So, if corn is your vegetable of choice, then you should plant corn with the expectancy of reaping a harvest of corn. Likewise, if you want a positive life, then you should be a positive person. However, if you don't put positivity into the universe, you won't get positivity from the universe, nor should you expect to.

CHAPTER 8

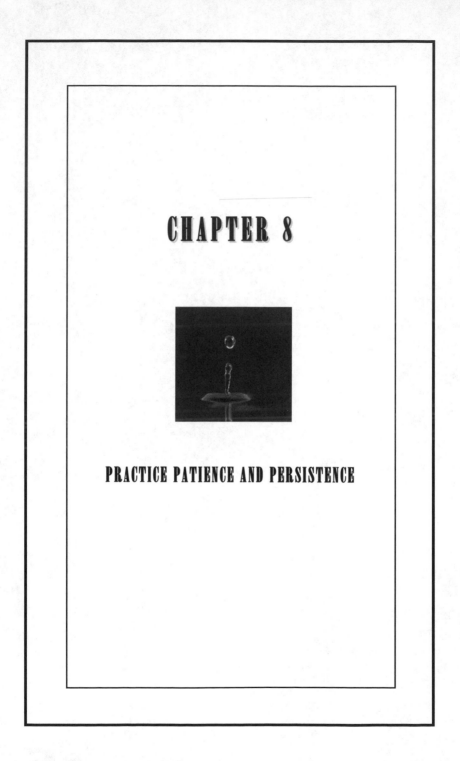

PRACTICE PATIENCE AND PERSISTENCE

"Baby...a slow drip will wear a hole in a rock." - Author Unknown

When I was young, I always thought that adults talked in riddles. Whenever I asked for an answer to a question, adults always gave me cryptic answers. Finally, I would stop asking. One of the people that was famous for conveying confusing thoughts was my grandmother. Whenever any of the kids were frustrated because we could not accomplish something, my grandmother would say, "Baby, a slow drip will wear a hole in a rock." To me, as a child, this was neither deep nor philosophical. Rather, it was one more perplexing concept that made me not want to communicate with adults. Over the years, I would come to hear this phrase many times, because I lack a sense of stick-to-it-ness. No matter how many times I hear it, clarity did not accompany it.

When I was in college and was struggling to write an important paper, I called my mother who was on her way out of town. She did not have time to chat, so I was referred to our family "psychologist," my grandmother. When I called her, I explained that I was working on a very important paper for school, but was suffering from writer's block. I told her that I feared that if I did not complete the paper I would not graduate. Despite my hysterics, she remained calm and repeated a familiar mantra, "Baby, a slow drip will wear a hole in a rock." Frustrated, I was polite and placated her by saying thank you and hanging up the phone. As I sat there at the computer (Dos Version), consumed with self-pity, her words resounded in my mind. Suddenly as if revelation were raining as manna from heaven, I got it. I said aloud, "A slow drip will wear a hole in a rock," at least three times. It dawned on me that I had learned in geology class that it was the slow, consistent and persistent dripping of water that eroded rock and created caves. I remember my professor saying that often the drip was slow, but the erosion was caused not by the speed of the water, by the unyielding, non-stop dripping.

At that moment, I realized that not only was my grandmother not "talking crazy," she was indeed brilliant. The message she was giving me would serve me well throughout the rest of my life. She was simply telling me not to give up and that I could accomplish my goals through persistence and consistency. And guess what? She didn't need a college degree to give me one of the most profound lessons that I would learn.

That day, two distinct things occurred that changed the course of my life. First, I began to practice the lesson that I have been taught that day, as a way of life. Second, I learned the difference between knowledge and wisdom. The information that my professor gave me about the evolution of the earth was knowledge. In and of itself, it held little relevance for my life, except maybe as an answer in a trivia game someday. My grandmother, on the other hand, had given me wisdom. She synthesized the knowledge with a practical application for life. This praxis has proven to be much more useful and valuable than all of the knowledge I have acquired for knowledge sake.

To everyone, but especially young people that are struggling in many areas of your lives, I want to let you know that the lesson of persistence and consistency is as relevant for your lives as it is for mine. Sometimes it seems as though adolescence will never end. The challenges that you face as you wrestle between childhood and adulthood to assert your independence, while simultaneously expecting parameters from your parents, can be overwhelming.

It occurred to me that we don't do a good job of teaching young people how to persevere through the difficult times. After hearing me speak at her school, a young lady emailed me and shared that she had attempted suicide and was unsuccessful. She was depressed and said, "I couldn't even commit suicide right." After affirming my delight in the fact that she was unsuccessful in her attempt, I asked her what would make a wonderful young lady like her want to kill herself. She told me that her father is a scientist and her brother is a doctor. Therefore, it is her family's expectation that she will do well in all of her subjects, but especially in science. She explained that she was having a difficult time learning the periodic table and as a result, she failed two major tests. I asked her if she had considered getting a tutor. She replied that she had worked with one for a couple of days, but could not get it. At that point, I asked her to tell me the greatest goal she had ever reached. She said she had never reached one goal that she had set for herself. She said, "I try lots of things, but I just don't get most things, so I quit."

During the course of the conversation, I realized that like me, she lacked a will to complete that which she started. I worked with her via email for about a year and a half. We started with her setting realistic goals. The first goal she set was passing the next science test with the aid of a tutor. She worked each day for the next three weeks leading up to the mid-term. Her tutor helped her to devise a system that she could understand and remember for learning the periodic table. She not only passed the test, but got a "B." Over the time that I served as her informal life coach, we took each exam one at a time and set goals along the way. Eventually, she developed a knack for finishing what she started. She said that from our time, she learned that long-term goals sometimes overwhelmed her, but that she could accomplish short and long-term goals, if she took it a little at a time. I reminded her that the key was not to think that everything in life would happen quickly. She had to be willing to be persistent in her efforts and not give up because things were challenging. As much as she learned from the experience, I think I learned even more. I was able to see how this principle, shared by a woman with a third grade education, was not only applicable to my life, but to that of a young person that I was mentoring.

It is important that you know that life will sometimes throw curve balls, which are called challenges or problems. Don't go back to the dugout without having swung the bat. Step up to the plate, plant your feet in the batter's box, focus your eye on the ball and swing. Even if you have two strikes, don't give up. Stand in the box and swing one more time. It's true that you could strike out. But you could also hit a home run. That home run will never happen if you give up because the curve ball seemed too great.

Be persistent and consistent and who knows, maybe you'll hit one of life's great home runs.

Remember that great people do not achieve great things by giving up. They are persistent in their effort and so you must also be. There is self-gratification in saying, "I've done it, I've completed my task." No matter the time it takes, stick to your goals. Keep working and don't quit, because a "slow drip wear a hole in rock." You are the drip and your challenge is the rock.

CHAPTER 9

YOU'LL NEVER LEARN TO SWIM IF YOU NEVER RISK DROWNING

"What would life be if we had no courage to try anything?" - Vincent van Gogh

I have met many people who live their lives with regret. Most often, they regret never taking risks to try new things. Most people are afraid of failing if they try new things. My philosophy is that you never have to worry about failing if you never try anything new. Each time we embark on a new adventure, we risk failure. But on the other side of that coin is the possibility of unimaginable success. I think that I have lived a rich life. Some of the choices I made were positive and netted me wonderful rewards. Other choices were negative and afforded me negative consequences. But each choice gave me more opportunities to know and grow as a human being, so I don't have many regrets.

As you know by now, I love doing nice things for my friends and trying new adventures. In 2001, I had the opportunity to do both at one time. My friend was working on her dissertation for completion of her Ph.D. Like many students, she procrastinated in writing and completing this document that overwhelmed her, yet occupied most of her conscious thoughts. As a way to ensure that she would indeed write and graduate without procrastination, I did three things. First, I told the teenagers with whom she volunteered that she was graduating and that they could come to see Bill Cosby as he was the commencement speaker. Next, I sent out invitations to her graduation party. Finally, I bought her a round-trip ticket to Hawaii. Needless to say, she felt pressured to finish. And she did. Two days after her commencement, we left for an 8-day trip to Maui.

When we arrived, we marveled at the beauty of the island. We got a rental car and to our chagrin were forced to rent what seemed like a clown car because it was so small. This is probably a good place to tell you that like me, my friend is also voluptuous, except she has eight more inches of height to add to her "voluptuosity". However, since it was the only car available, we decided to cope and adjust. I believe we said that it looked like Hawaii was God's canvas, whereon he painted his earthly masterpiece. After checking into the hotel, we started to plan our itinerary for the week. Immediately, we saw a plethora of brochures for activity packages. My friend was content to just travel around to see the tourist sites and go to popular restaurants on the island. I immediately began to look at packages that included things like scuba diving, parasailing, paddleboating and jet skiing.

The first few days were filled with "touristy" site visits to see volcanic mountains, beaches, and sites of indigenous people of the island. We ate foods that were unique to Hawaii and bought as many souvenirs as we could for our friends and family. We both agreed that before we left, wanted to visit the famous "Road to Hana." That road is famous because it had so many zig-zags, turns and spirals that there is a T-shirt that reads, "I Survived the Road to Hana."

On the 4th day, we decided to go across the island to try our hand at jet skiing. I was surprised that my friend agreed to try it, too. When we got out to the boat dock, we were given instructions such as how to get back on the ski if we fell off, how far out we could go in the ocean and how to drive a jet ski. The instructors asked us to do a trial run to be sure we could handle the ski. When I took mine out, I'll admit I was a little wobbly. OK, I looked like an alcoholic on a tight wire. So they advised that we should take one ski out and that my friend should drive. Although I agreed, I have to admit that I wondered if the jet ski could hold both of us. When they said yes, all I could think was, "We are going to put a hurtin' on this ski." We climbed aboard. They attached my friend's life jacket to the ignition of the jet ski. It was explained that if she were to fall of the jet ski, it would turn off the ignition. When I got on, I held on to her life jacket as I was instructed to do.

I cautioned my friend that if I fell off, she too would fall off. Finally, we were off.

We were having a great time. After we turned each curve, I asked her to speed up. As we approached a curve, I asked her to slow down. We went through this routine for about 40 minutes. We both were having a great time. With about five minutes to go before the end of our time, we were going at top speed as we rounded a curve and hit a wave. I remember screaming, "I'm falling offffffffffffffffff!" I went high into the air and hit the water with an impact that was so hard that it knocked my life jacket and $25 goggles off.

So, there I was floating in the middle of the ocean without a life jacket. As a child, I was a competitive swimmer, so I wasn't afraid of drowning. But, I assumed if I yelled that I was drowning, I would get a faster response from guys at the dock. So, I yelled, "I'm drowwwwwwwwning!" I began to use the swimming technique for staying afloat called treading water. Suddenly an odd thought ran across my mind. I suddenly realized that I did not see my friend, which meant she had not fallen in. I know I should have been happy that she was OK, but I reverted back to childhood and was ticked off that she had not fallen in, too. So, I started yelling, "help, I'm drowning!"

From about twenty-five feet behind me, I heard my friend's voice say, "Tei, I'm over here." I turned around and lo and behold I saw my friend in the water. Before you think it, yes, I know that it is sick that all of a sudden I felt better to know that she was in the water, too. I swam over to her. When I finally reached her, I was out of breath because I am a big girl who had not swam in many, many years. It was upon my arrival that she informed me that she could not swim. I thought, "Oh great, I have no life jacket and you have no swimming skills." I told her it was OK because she had a life jacket and I could tread water. As my legs began to kick in an attempt to keep me afloat, it suddenly occurred to me that this summer had been the summer of sharks attacking people in the oceans. Immediately, my mind went into panic mode. On every Jaws movie I had ever seen, it was when someone was kicking their legs that the shark was drawn to them. All I could think was, "Man, with both of our big butts out here in the ocean, Jaws will have a feast."

I could just imagine him whistling to his friends saying, "Fellows, come on and bring your families; this is a smorgasbord." At this thought, the humor in my mind turned to fear and panic.

I turned to my friend to share my thoughts and fears. Then I asked about the location of the jet ski. We looked out and saw that it was about 100 yards away from us. Indeed the motor had shut down when she fell off, but the waves and currents carried it away from her. So, here we were, one of us who could not swim and the other who knew how to swim, but was too fat and out of shape to swim 100 yards. Since I did not see anyone coming for us, I decided to swim for it and she decided to doggy paddle toward it. After what seemed like a half hour (was actually only a few minutes), we finally reached the jet ski. During our instructions, we were told that if we were to fall off we should pull ourselves up from the back of the vehicle. So, I tried to pull myself up, but to no avail, because my arms were staging a revolt for the abuse I had already heaped on them during the swim. As I tried to pull all of my voluptuosity up on the ski, it occurred to me that the bulge under my arm that gave me 5 more seconds on my wave was not a muscle, it was flab. Once again, I slid back in the water. Finally, I got the idea to try to help my friend pull herself up. Although she was larger than I (5'8, 250lbs), she was also stronger. After several attempts, we gave up and decided to wait for the life guards to come help us.

Soon, we saw a jet ski coming toward us. We were relieved that help was on the way. That is, until we saw the help. The guy who came out was a young, blond, white kid who was no more than 5'7", weighing about 135 pounds soaking wet. When he came out, he got in the water and decided to try to help my friend first. He positioned himself under her in an effort to try to hoist her upward. I think he bought the myth that we are weightless in water. My friend and I both had T-shirts on over our swim suits. In case you don't know, a swim suit on a fat chick is like a thong. So, as he went under her, he had two BIG brown cheeks in his face as he emerged from under the water. I am sure he was thinking, "They don't pay me enough for this. Today is my last day!"

She had the look of embarrassment and disgust on her face as she demanded that he "STOP!" She decided that she would work on her own to get herself back on. So, he moved to me. The view under me was not any better than under her. He'd push up and I'd slide back down. Each attempt made me swallow more ocean water, which was beginning to make me nauseous. Just as I was getting my fill of him too, the ultimate stereotypical surfer dude came to our rescue.

This 6'2", long, blond-haired guy with great pectoral muscles pulled up beside our jet ski. He said to my friend, "Dude, I'm gonna reach over, grab your hand and pull you up. So, he stood on his jet ski as a brace, reached for my friend's hand as she was in the water, and pulled her onto the jet ski. At that point, he instructed her to go back to the deck and wait for me. Instead, she refused to leave me and only drove a few feet away. Now it was my turn. He tried the same thing, but there was a hitch. My arms were much shorter than my friend's and would not reach his. Looking back it was quite comical, but then I was cold, scared and sick. Finally, he got on his jet ski and pulled me up. I was elated, but now I had to drive myself back to the deck following my friend. Couple the fact that the exhaust from her ski was blowing into my face with the fact that I looked like an alcoholic trying to steer the ski and you get a severely nauseous woman.

When we finally reached the deck, the guy who had been taking photos decided that the events were funny and said, laughing, "What happened out there, you fall off?" At that moment, the contents of my stomach and the sea water all came rushing up as I barfed all over him.

I felt very ill all the way to the car, so my friend agreed to drive back to the hotel. We looked at the map and discovered that there was a shorter way to get back to our hotel, so that I could lie down. Or so we thought. We began the new path back to the hotel. About half way into our journey, we discovered that we were on the mountain/road that led to Hana. The road had two-way traffic, but was only wide enough to accommodate one vehicle at a time. So, if another car was coming in the opposite direction, we would have to get really close to the mountain to let them pass. This, along with the fact that I had to stop every 10 minutes to throw up made for a very long trip up and down the mountain (2 hours versus 35 minutes the other way).

When we got back to the hotel, I just wanted to lie down. My friend asked me if I regretted having tried jet skiing. I looked at her and said with all honesty, "Absolutely not. If we had not gone, you would not have known that you could swim and I would not have known the thrill of going 120 miles an hour on the water with the wind in my face. Also, each of us has a new adventure under our belts. None of that would have been possible, if we had never tried. And besides, we have a great story to tell our friends."

The moral of my story is that you have to be willing to try new things if you are ever going to grow beyond your comfort zone. But for sure, each time you risk trying something new, you risk failing. However nothing beats a failure, but a try. If you never try, you are already defeated. I have lived a fun-filled, rich life with many varied experiences. Each experience has taught me a valuable lesson, whether it was positive or negative. That is the reason that I have such a diverse perspective on life and am open to the possibilities that life has a lot to offer us, if only we'll take healthy risks.

One thing is for sure - you'll never learn to swim if you don't risk drowning.

Chapter 10

WHEN I DARE TO BE POWERFUL

"When I dare to be powerful - to use my strength in the service of my vision, then it becomes less and less important whether I am afraid" – Audre Lorde

There is an old Jewish proverb told to me by my college roommate, David, that states, "I have been through the fire and what fire does not consume it hardens/strengthens." Today in church, the pastor spoke of fire as a purifier that produces, if it does not destroy it, the best part of the thing placed therein. Well, I can attest that in my life, it has been the difficult things that I have faced which have made me stronger and a better person. I must admit that in the midst of my personal fires, I can honestly say that at no time during those tumultuous times did I rejoice in the knowledge that I would be better for having experienced them.

Today, I tell young people what the end result of hard times will be for them emotionally, spiritually and sometimes physically. But in doing so, I never lose sight of the fact that it is easy to give advice when you are not the person who is going through the pain, hardship and tough times. This chapter is for those who are "going through" and are not quite sure of the benefits. As you successfully navigate each storm of your life, you will find that it is the navigation through which you learn and grow. It is the storm that makes us strong. Through strength, we gain a greater sense of our own personal power. So, each time you face your storm head on you "dare to be powerful." I say dare because some people opt out and give up, but you dare to believe that you can rise above any situation. So, if for no other reason, stay in the game of life because you dare life to keep coming at you and each time you face it, you say, in the words of legendary rocker, Pat Benatar, "Hit Me With Your Best Shot."

Recently, I had an opportunity to join a national organization. During the process for gaining membership into the organization, the road was filled with many bumps. There were certainly times when I wondered if I would be able to sustain all the rigor of the process. Perhaps the worst part of it all was that during the entire time, I was made to feel that I was not worthy of membership, that I was not worthy of labeling myself a Christian and the fact that some people maligned my character. I have always prided myself on the fact that I am a strong, African American woman with a high tolerance for emotional pain. Yet, at least twice per week, I found myself reduced to tears from the personal attacks, lies and misperceptions heaped on me by those who were my peers and those already in the organization. I have always possessed the greatest respect for the organization and wanted membership so badly that I could taste it. So, for the longest time, I suffered in silence.

I knew that I was not a quitter and that ultimately the goal was be to stay in the game. If I could just keep my eyes on the prize, I could get through even this. I would love to tell you that I triumphed with no emotional scars, but that would be a lie and I have made it a point not to lie to kids. I did eventually gain membership into the organization, but I am still removing some of the mental scar tissue left behind. But, I can tell you that the process made me explore my own strengths and weaknesses and made me do some long overdue introspection. This introspection forced me to see things in my personality that were less than desirable.

Through the process, God (and some good friends) helped me to learn that I lacked humility, which is a necessary quality for beings a good servant to God and to your fellow human beings. I always thought I possessed humility, but I quickly learned that I was kidding myself, and a few others who didn't know any better. This revelation helped me to grow as a Christian and as a person. Further, I learned the importance of forgiveness. Through the lessons of humility, I was able to recognize that I was in need of forgiveness for the transgressions (real or perceived) that I committed against others. Further, I needed forgiveness from God for those times during the process when I was not a good witness of who God is.

Finally, I was taught the lesson of forgiveness for those who had transgressed against me. I learned that when I forgave others, it gave me the freedom to worship God without bondage. It also, enabled me to heal some of the wounds. So, though the process into membership was painful and trying, I can honestly say that I am grateful for the process, the pain, the turmoil, but most importantly, I am grateful for the lessons. The organization, its history and its members are part of this nation's history and its destiny. I feel honored to now be a part of this illustrious organization.

A couple of days ago, I had the opportunity to do a speech for a Girl Power overnight in Northeastern Ohio. To my surprise and delight the young women were well versed in the knowledge of themselves in general and in the history of women's rights in specific. I quickly realized that these young women were not in need of a Girl Power speech, but a Woman Power speech. As we began to dialogue, it became evident that many of the young women were struggling with tough issues, many of which surpassed the usual high school "stuff." Some of them talked about their futures with a sense of doom, gloom and hopelessness. They believed that because their lives had been tough so far, there was no reason to expect that things would miraculously change for the better.

The sense of hopelessness expressed by the young ladies saddened me at first. Then it occurred to me that I could turn their knowledge of women's history into an applicable, teachable moment. I asked them to recount the historical events from which an admiration of the women of history emerged for them. They recounted the Suffrage Movement, the Great Depression, the Civil Rights Movement, the fight for Roe v. Wade and a host of other events that made them proud of women. I asked, "Do you think the women of history had smooth sailing as they set out to challenge the status quo and change the course of history?"

After some contemplation, they all responded "No!"

I replied, "Then what makes you think there won't be rough times as you navigate the waters of your life? It is the survivors of the storms that tell the stories, not the condition of their boats." The lesson is that you can expect tough times in your life, because that is a natural part of living. However, it is when you come through those times with courage and lessons learned that you really have a chance to see what you are made of. I guarantee you that if you weather each storm of your life without giving up, you will be stronger, wiser and bolder for the experience!

CHAPTER 11

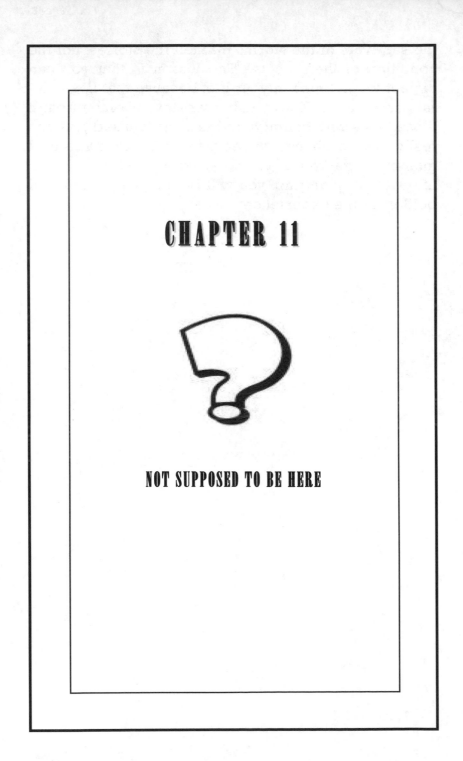

NOT SUPPOSED TO BE HERE

"Mercy is getting a second chance when you don't deserve it." -Veggie Tales Movie

Have you ever wondered why you are on Earth? If you have, I can assure you that you are not alone. I think that each of us has explored the question at least once, if only in our mind. I believe we are each here with a unique purpose to fulfill. If you are like me, you learn early what your purpose is, but you spend the majority of your life running from it and trying to convince yourself that you don't really know why you are here.

For most of my adult life I have known that God had big plans for me and my life. He wanted to use me to tell people about His Son and about His goodness and what He wants for mankind. Although I had this knowledge, most of what I did in my life was the polar opposite of what God wanted me to do. If He said go right, I went left. If He said help your neighbor, I helped myself. If He said speak, I was silent. I was so scared that if I lived a God-inspired life, my peers would reject me. So, instead, I rejected God and His will for my life.

A few years ago, my life appeared to be going well to most of the outside world. I used the "life is perfect" façade to deceive the masses. Outwardly, my life looked good. I had a job at which I was successful, associates by the bushel, a company that was thriving. Yet, I was miserable on the inside. I was hollow, empty and secretly self-destructive. There were many days and nights that I lay awake contemplating how to end my life in a way that would not be painful or obvious. The one thing that kept me from committing suicide, however, was my spiritual belief that suicide was an unforgivable sin and that I would leave this world and spend eternity in hell. So, I would trudge through each day with a smile on my face and immeasurable pain in my heart. The hardest part was the knowledge that there was a cure for what ailed me. All I needed to do was call on God and ask Him to help me, but even then, something kept me from asking Him.

I was at a Teen Institute Retreat for a school called Nordonia. I was there as a staff member instead of a speaker, which afforded me the opportunity to relax with the students. That Sunday, I went to the Spiritual Sharing (optional) part of the retreat. My friends, Heidi and Renaldo, were leading the service. When the students solicited prayer requests, I began to cry uncontrollably and asked them to keep me in their prayers. I left the retreat and returned to my nice little home, in my nice little city, on my nice little street. For the rest of the evening, I could not muster a smile because I could not hide the truth from myself. I was woefully unhappy and only one thing could change that. I went to bed with the heaviest heart I had ever known.

The next morning, many schools were closed, though the weather was fine. One of the schools that was closed was the one at which my sister was a teacher. On my way to the bathroom, I grabbed my phone so that I could call her to congratulate her on an extra day off. I told her of the crying episode the day before, and as I did, I felt a deep yearning to end the pain with which I had chosen to be saddled for so many years. Suddenly, I told my sister that it was time. She began to pray first for me and then with me. It was that morning, on the toilet, that I asked Jesus to come into my heart and to forgive me for my sins. I can honestly say that that was the most peace I had ever known or felt.

I spent the next couple years living a life that finally felt like it was worth living. I continued to work a job that I liked, surrounded myself with friends and associates who demonstrated their care and concern for me. I walked with God and He with me. I thought that was all that I needed to do, and technically, I was right. All that was required for me to have a good life was a surrender of my life to Christ, which I had done. And though my life was happy, I was still missing something. I knew that God had blessed me with many gifts and that he had called me to use those gifts to help others. I thought that my community service work, my job and my willingness to do outreach to those in need were enough because it was all good work. But I read a book called The Purpose Driven Life, that helped to make the distinction for me. In a chapter on which I became fixated, it read, "Not every good work is God's work." Still, I persisted in my path of ignorance to God's will for my life. However, make no mistake, if you ignore God long enough, He has a way of getting your attention.

October 15, 2004; that was the day that God got my attention with a special wake up call. I had been at the Columbus Youth Commission's Youth Summit since about 7:15 a.m. At the conclusion of the day, I was excited to get home, change clothes and prepare to go to a high school football game with one of my friends. At about 5:00, I said goodbye to the commissioners and advised them to be careful because it was raining and I had heard on the radio that there were lots of accidents. Just before I pulled off, I stopped to give Heidi a sweater because it was cool outside and she had on short sleeves. As I got back in my car, something, (The Holy Spirit) told me to put my seatbelt on. Now, that might not mean anything to most people, but everyone who knows me well, knows that I do not wear a seatbelt. (Years ago, my half sister was in an accident and as she was struggling to get out of her seatbelt, the car exploded, killing her. That scared me for a lifetime.)

But, that day, I listened to the voice in my head and put my seatbelt on.

I was careful not to go fast as the road was very wet and traffic appeared to be moving slowly. I had just left the outer-belt and had merged onto the main highway that would take me home. Suddenly, I saw a purple vehicle coming in my direction across the grass. When I turned to look to my left, it was a purple pick-up truck that was coming at my driver's side door. He was coming so fast that there was no time to change lanes. He hit my door with such force that it caused the car to spin out of control. I put my left arm up to guard my face and held onto the steering wheel with my right hand. I began to scream, "Jesus!" In what was a couple of seconds, but seemed like a couple of minutes, my car was spinning out of control, knocking down a chain link fence. At that moment, the car began to flip down an embankment, through trees. My screams were timed with each bounce. I yelled, "Jesus!" — boom— "Please forgive me!" —boom— "For anything I have done that is not like you, please forgive me!" —final boom. As my car landed, right-side up, all I could feel was elation at the fact that I was alive. I began to say aloud, "Thank you Jesus for letting me be alive." I didn't care that it was not the most well-constructed sentence that I had ever put together. The only thing I cared about was the fact that at the bottom of this embankment, in a smashed up car, was me - ALIVE!

Once I realized that I was alive, the adrenaline really kicked in, as did my comic relief factor. I tried to open my driver's side door to no avail. The door was too damaged to open. As I established earlier in the book, I am definitely a voluptuous woman. I don't know if it was the adrenaline or what, but I got the bright idea to try to climb out of the driver's side window. And why not? There was no glass left in the window. I soon learned that you cannot get a 4' x 6' butt out of a 2' x 3' window. I was able to get a leg (with no shoe) out of the window, only to find my foot stuck in a muddy pond. I pulled my foot back in.

At that point, I felt an excruciating pain emanate from my lower back and down my left leg. The pain caused me to wince aloud. Then, I saw a young man racing down the hill. He informed me that he had called 911. He instructed me to unlock the passenger door. I reached across and it was at that point that I realized that I could not move my left leg. Soon, another guy (Dale Butts) came down. He opened my door and as I was on my back, I was now laying out of the car. He squatted beneath me and agreed to hold me up until the emergency squad arrived. And he did. I'll bet he would not have made that pledge if he had known that it was going to take the squad forty minutes to arrive. I have to confess that for the first fifteen of those minutes, the only thing I could focus on was where my cell phone might be. This is a good time to tell you that I am wedded to my cell phone. They found it on the hill. Like most of the stuff in my car, it flew out of the window when I was flipping down the embankment.

While we were waiting for the emergency squad, the same gentleman who had called 911 agreed to call anyone I'd like. I asked him to call my friend Heidi, because I had just left her, so I knew that she would get there quickly. I wanted the comfort of being around someone who would both comfort and pray for me. When he made the call, he was so calm as he told Heidi that he was there with her friend Tei who had been in a bad accident. Because I had just left her, coupled with his calm made Heidi believed he was joking and she said, "Yeah right." At that point, I started screaming in the background, "Heidi, it's me!"

I could hear her panic set in as she said, "Where is she? Is she alright?"

The young man told her where the accident was and said, "It's pretty bad." I think that is when I started to get nervous. Prior to this, I could feel pain in my left leg and left side of my back. I could see that my brand new (had just purchased it in Vegas) Delta Sigma Theta, tan & burgundy jacket was torn on the sleeve. I could not see what the men could see; that I was badly cut and was bleeding.

As we were still waiting for the emergency squad, I asked if he would call my friend and Soror, Dionne. I wanted him to call her because though she lives in Cincinnati, she had been at the Youth Summit and had left us about 45 minutes before my accident. We were scheduled to meet later in the evening to attend a high school football game. I gave him the number and he dialed. When she answered, he explained that her friend Tei had been in an accident and that Heidi was on her way. She said somewhat nonchalantly, "OK."

Again, I began screaming, "Dionne, it's me!" She later told me that because he was so calm, she assumed I had had a fender bender and that Heidi was picking me up. She assumed that I was with police and would call her later. Once she realized it was serious and had gotten directions, she was on her way to the scene.

After about 25 minutes and the squad had not arrived, another call was placed to 911. They indicated that the squad had been dispatched to 270 & 70 on the East Side and we were on the west side, so they had to redirect them during rush hour traffic. About that same time, Heidi arrived and was coming down the hill with the executive director of the Community Relations Commission. When they reached me, I could tell from the look on their faces that something was wrong that I could not see. But, Mr. Stowe, who is also a minister, prayed for me. His prayer brought a calm to my spirit and seemed to ease a little of the pain that I was feeling in my left side. This would be a good time to note that my other hero, Dale Butts, was still squatting beneath me, holding me up. I turned to him as he joked and said, "If it helps you any, I can't feel my legs." We both laughed and remarked about the slowness of the emergency squad.

Finally, after 40 minutes the emergency squad and the police arrived. The first guys on the scene rushed down the hill. I could hear them talking to each other. One said, "We're gonna have to cut back the trees to get the basket down here to get her out." A couple of minutes later, one of the firefighters came down to tell me not to be alarmed, because they were going to use a chainsaw to cut some of the trees back. The sound of the chainsaw did not bother me, but the fumes from the exhaust were nauseating.

Once they finished cutting back the trees, the time came to figure out how they were going to get me out of the car. They realized that the incline was too great to bring the stretcher down the hill. So, they decided to bring the stiff board and a basket. The humor in my head started to run wild as I saw the facial expressions of the first paramedics who came down the hill with the board, when they saw how large I was. They sent a nonverbal signal back up the hill that they were definitely going to need reinforcements.

They came to the car and asked Dale to move so that they could try to position the stiff board underneath me. When they tried to put it under me, my body writhed with pain and I shrieked. I explained that I could not move the left side of my lower body. They were very cautious as they slid the board under me. The next step was to get the neck brace on as a preventative measure. They had a problem getting it on because I don't have a neck. They tried different collars and soon discovered that they did not have one that would work, so they made a make-shift collar. Once my neck was secured, they began the really funny part - finding a way to get me on the board, into the basket and up the hill. It took 5 men to get me from the car into the basket. They were straining and sweating the entire time.

Once they had me in the basket, then came the task of getting me up the hill. Since it was raining and the hill was muddy, it was extra slippery. Once the five para-medics had me out of the car, they signaled for assis-tance from two other medics that were at the top of the hill. So, now there were seven people all straining to get me up the hill. I looked at them and said, "Sure hope you guys had your Wheaties today." They chuckled, which made me nervous because they needed all the strength and focus they could muster to get me up that hill.

As I got to the top of the hill, I saw Dionne and I heard a familiar voice. As I looked to the left, I saw a fuchsia sweater, worn by my Sands, W. Shawna Gibbs who said, "I'm here, Sands." As they were putting me into the squad, I heard her say, "I wanna see the car." As soon as she did, she started screaming, "Oh LAWD" at the site of the car, until Dionne reminded her, "Shawna, Tei is not in the car."

Once in the squad, 5 paramedics worked on me. I have to admit that I was terribly uncomfortable to be lying there as they began to cut my pants off of me. Then, they cut my jacket off and my nice new brown suede shirt. I know those are material things, but I real-ly liked that whole outfit and it was very expensive. My Cole Haan shoes had already come off in the accident and now I was losing my designer outfit, too. There I was, in only my panties and bra as five white guys poked and prodded me. To assuage my discomfort of having my fat and flab open before those men, I cracked a joke which put us all at ease. I said, "Well, look at it this way fellows. When you go home, you can tell your kids that you got to see Shamu and you didn't even have to go to Sea World." We all laughed. The laughter helped to take my mind off of the intense pain I felt as we hit what seemed like a million bumps en route to the hospital.

Once I reached the hospital I was transferred into the care of the trauma team. This in and of itself frightened me. Each person who looked at my arm made a face, so I knew it had to be bad. I won't tell you how traumatic my ER experience was, but I will tell you that they added insult to injury when they could not find my vein to give me an IV and then to top it off, they cut my brand new $32 bra off. I had been jovial until that point. Now I was truly depressed. The bedside manner of the trauma team, the x-ray technicians and the ER Nurses left a lot to be desired. I had proposed in my heart that if I had to be admitted, I was going to phone my primary physician to have her request a transfer. No way would I spend a night there.

While I was laying in the ER waiting to see the doctor so he could stitch up my arm and tell me if I had a fractured pelvis, a nurse came to tell me that there were a lot of people waiting to see me. She said I could only see one at a time and asked who I wanted to see first. Because Dionne has my medical power of attorney, I had listed her as my sister and next of kin. I did not list my parents or my real sister because I am estranged from them. So, in about two minutes, my Sands, W., came back. She said, "Girl, everybody is here." I wanted to know who, and she responded in typical fashion,

"Er'body." I asked her if she would get a nurse because I needed a bed pan as I had not used the bathroom since 7:00 a.m. and it was now 8:30 p.m. The nurse told her I would have to wait. I had to go really badly, so Shawna found a bedpan for me. Because I could not move my left side, I could not get my underwear down to get on the bedpan. Despite my protestations, she helped me. Then she slid the bedpan underneath me. She asked if I was on. I could only feel 1/2 of my body, so I assumed I was on. As I started to pee, I quickly learned that only half of me was on. One half went in the bedpan and one half went in the bed. She told the nurse that I needed my sheets changed. They made me wait 15 minutes before they came to change my sheets.

Once they did, I was flooded with visitors, including Heidi and Dionne, my parents and my Aunt Marion, Jim Stowe, my other Sands, Quiona, my Specs, Terina and Kimberly, Kim's niece, Kiara, and her friend, Robert, who had just flown in from D.C. Finally, after about 5 hours, the doctor came back to clean out the wound and sew my arm up. I asked to see a mirror, because I wanted to see what had made everyone gasp. When I saw it, I understood that the wound was 5 inches wide and about 11 inches long. My tissue was hanging out, as was my flab. It was the flab that kept my tendons from being severed. First time fat ever came in handy. J I watched and talked with the surgeon as he sewed my arm taking pride in his handiwork.

When I was finished at about 12:30, everyone was still there. Dionne took me to get my meds and my Sorors met me at the house to help me in since I could not walk. Over the course of the next two weeks, my friends made sure that I had everything that I needed, including a walker. Heidi came daily to change my dressings and bring me comfortable pillows. My Sands and Specs made sure I had food daily, and that I could get to appointments with my doctors and attorney. Though I was incapacitated for a couple of weeks, I learned how much I am loved during this period.

My survival from the accident really helped me to understand something much bigger than my mind could fully comprehend. GOD had big plans for my life and he had spared me so that I could complete his will for my life. I want to spend my life helping people, young and old, realize their best lives. Part of it will be fulfilled when I enroll in and complete seminary. I knew years ago that I was supposed to spread the gospel of Jesus Christ to the masses. The other part of my fulfilling God's will for my life includes expanding my motivational speaking on a larger scale. I am ever mindful that none of this is about me. That has been the greatest lesson I have learned. Surviving the kind of accident that I did showed me that I am nothing on my own. I was forced to rely on God for my every need, including life. That's all God really desires from each of us. To rely solely on Him for absolutely EVERYTHING! So, hopefully you won't have to go through something as tragic as a car accident for God to get your attention.

The moral of this story is that, according to man's calculations, I am not supposed to be here. Under normal circumstances I would have died in that accident, down that embankment. But there is nothing "Normal" about GOD. He is Supernatural. So, in His estimation, I am still supposed to be here. However, my survival comes with a cost, as does yours. If we are on Earth and we don't do something to leave the world a better place than when arrive, we are just taking up space in the universe. My advice to each of you is to stop talking about change and start doing change. Don't talk about it, be about it. The best way to do this is to find your purpose and your passion and walk in it! I CHARGE YOU WITH IT!!!!!

The Amazing Tei Street by